CONCEPTS OF
SELF AND MORALITY

CONCEPTS OF SELF AND MORALITY

Women's Reasoning about Abortion

Judith G. Smetana

PRAEGER

PRAEGER SPECIAL STUDIES • PRAEGER SCIENTIFIC

Library of Congress Cataloging in Publication Data

Smetana, Judith G., 1951-
　　Concepts of self and morality.

　　Bibliography: p.
　　Includes indexes.
　　1. Abortion—United States—Psychological
aspects.　2. Abortion—United States—Moral
and religious aspects.　3. Women—United States
—Attitudes.　4. Adolescent girls—United States
—Attitudes.　I. Title.
HQ767.5.U5S73　　　363.4′6　　　　　81-13807
ISBN 0-03-057703-9　　　　　　　　　AACR2

Published in 1982 by Praeger Publishers
CBS Educational and Professional Publishing
a Division of CBS Inc.
521 Fifth Avenue, New York, New York 10175 U.S.A.

© 1982 by Praeger Publishers

23456789　145　987654321

Printed in the United States of America

Foreword by
ELLIOT TURIEL

Occasionally, research serves the dual function of informing us about a topic of great social importance, as well as advancing our understanding of theoretical issues. The research program discussed in this book rests on sound social-scientific methods and stems from a concern with theory-based issues pertaining to social cognition. Professor Smetana has investigated parsimoniously several problems of longstanding interest in the field of social cognition. Her research incorporates the study of social concepts, the coordination of different domains of social reasoning, the relations between social concepts and action, and women's (and, to a lesser extent, men's) reasoning about the issue of terminating or continuing a pregnancy. By studying social reasoning, important contributions are made to an understanding of the topic of abortion; by studying the topic of abortion, important contributions are made to knowledge about social reasoning and behavior.

The position taken in this book, consistent with traditions among some social and developmental psychologists, is that thinking, reflection, and decision making are all central elements in social functioning. This research continues that tradition and extends it in new and interesting directions. The author's position is most closely linked with an approach to the structure and development of thought stimulated largely by the theories of Jean Piaget. Analyses of the development of social judgments, going back to Piaget's early and influential work in The Moral Judgment of the Child, have been aimed primarily at uncovering the nature of social reasoning and social inference. Researchers have, for good reasons, concentrated on the study of thinking about general domains of social knowledge (such as morality, rules, law, authority, social institutions, political systems, social convention), rather than specific substantive topics (such as abortion, capital punishment, racial prejudice). For the most part, psychological studies of specific topics, and especially complex or ambiguous ones, have been limited to surveys of attitudes and assessment of associated background variables, such as social class and religious affiliation.

A topic like abortion is especially problematic for analyses of social reasoning because it is highly contested. Even within a culture one finds little consensus and much heated disputation. The contested nature of the topic and the fact that the disputants can rarely convince each other through argumentation give the appearance that we are in the realm of the nonrational—or even the irrational, since discussions are often emotionally charged. Without denying the emotionality stirred by the issue or the seeming intransigence of positions, Professor Smetana has shown the significance of social reasoning in people's decisions regarding abortion; the complexities and ambiguities of this issue have provided her with a means for studying this process. Starting with the proposition that judgments about abortion are not of one kind, Professor Smetana has made novel extensions of previous research paradigms to analyze the mixture of categories in those judgments.

The research began with a sound epistemological strategy, namely, careful identification and definition of the components of the problem. Professor Smetana posits that two categories of social judgment—the moral and the personal—are most salient in the reasoning of the women in her samples. People are not typed. The claim is not that moral judgment characterizes some women, while personal reasoning characterizes other women. Rather, the claim is that all the women were capable of and engaged in both kinds of judgments, but that they differed in their classifications of abortion as a moral or a personal issue (evidence is presented that the women's general type or level of moral judgment was not a distinguishing factor).

The conceptual categories stem from recent research, with which I and several others have been involved, showing that social reasoning can be usefully delineated according to domains of knowledge (for example, moral judgments, concepts of systems of social organization and convention, psychological concepts of others and self). A study closely related to this research on abortion was conducted by Larry Nucci. Nucci found that children and adolescents consider social regulation legitimate for certain social actions—in some cases for moral reasons, in other cases for reasons of convention. There is, however, a realm of social action that is considered the prerogative of personal decision and that, therefore, should not be regulated by either formal (for example, law) or informal (for example, custom, convention) means.

The focus of most of the research we have done thus far, including Nucci's study, has been on prototypical examples of social actions within domains of social judgment. Prototypical examples are used in order to ascertain the conceptual criteria applicable to each domain. Of course, not all social issues or social conflicts take the character of domain-specific prototypical examples. Some issues are not prototypical, with ambiguities stemming from the merging of more than one domain. One of the insights of Professor Smetana's research was the recognition that complex and ambiguous issues may be systematically related to the process of coordinating more than one domain. It may be that the complexities and ambiguities stemming from category mixture are, in turn, sources of strong divisions regarding appropriate courses of action. The contested nature of the issue, the imperviousness of positions to argumentation from those taking an opposing position may be related, in part, to the substantive presence of more than one of the fundamental domains of social knowledge. The power of the analyses in this book can be seen in the explication of divergent conceptualizations about the same problem. It is clear that conceptualizations are involved. One of the intriguing findings is that some people conceptualize abortion as a moral issue and some conceptualize it as a nonmoral issue.

The data presented can be read from two perspectives. The data were gathered using an interview procedure that is systematic, guided by specific hypotheses, and designed to provide sufficiently rich information to enable descriptions of processes of judgment. Piaget has referred to this type of interview method as a form of experimentation in that hypotheses are tested with structured questions and a constant attempt is made to control for the interviewee's interpretations of tasks and questions. On the one hand, the interview responses were subjected to analyses through carefully and precisely formulated coding categories that constitute objective and reliable descriptions of social judgments. On the other hand, the presentation of a good number of interview excerpts provides the reader with rich and vivid examples of women's reasoning about abortion. For many of the women the discussions were more than academic, since they were confronting the decision of whether or not to continue their pregnancies. From these interviews we learn a great deal about opinions and attitudes toward abortion by going beyond the surface level of an assessment of approval or disapproval of the act to the level of assumptions and processes of reasoning. We learn what makes for the attitudes and thereby obtain greater understanding of those attitudes.

I have said that by studying the topic of abortion contributions are made to knowledge of a theoretical nature. One contribution comes from the analyses of the coordination of domains of reasoning on a multifaceted and complex social problem. A second and equally important contribution comes from that aspect of the research dealing with the relations of social judgments and actions. Our tendency is to assume a straightforward relation, or lack of it, between thought and action. We are prone to ask questions like, "Do people live up to their moral values?" or "Are people's actions consistent with their moral judgments?" These questions are translated into a social-scientific approach to the problem of thought and action. Debates are waged over the answers to these questions. Some argue that large discrepancies exist between behavior and verbally espoused values or moral judgments. Others argue that moral judgments guide action, making for close relations between the two. Both sides are able to point to supporting research evidence. The usual research procedure is to obtain two measures, one of moral judgment and one of be-havior, and to assess their degree of correspondence. The results of these studies have varied considerably, thus allowing the claim of supporting research evidence by both those who believe there is a re-lation and those who believe there is a discrepancy between moral judgment and behavior. In other words, some studies show high cor-respondence and other studies show low correspondence between the two measures.

The research procedures are usually correlational in concep-tion, with the overriding question posed being a predictive one: How predictive is judgment of behavior? It seems to me that a reconcep-tualization of the relations between thought and action is needed. Rather than assuming a causal relation from judgment to action, we should consider the ways in which systems of social judgment are coordinated with systems of action. Rather than using action as the variable judgment predicts to, it should be regarded as a component in coordinations of conceptual and action systems. Many studies in-volving behavioral decisions call for more than one type of social judgment. Situations that involve moral judgments are also likely to include components entailing nonmoral social judgments—such as pragmatic or social-institutional considerations. Accordingly, ex-planations of the relations of judgment and behavior require an under-standing of how domains of social judgment are coordinated. By con-sidering the relation of only one type of judgment (for example, moral-ity) to behavioral outcomes, other relevant social judgments are omitted; misleading conclusions may, therefore, be drawn regarding the general relations of thought and action.

The findings reported by Professor Smetana point to the impor-tance of investigating the coordination of domains of social judgment in behavioral decisions. The design of the research permitted com-parisons of behavioral decisions to varying interpretations of the event. Close correspondences were found between judgment and ac-tion; a woman's conceptualization of the event as personal or moral corresponded with the decision to continue or terminate the pregnancy. If the study had been designed to relate level of moral judgment to the behavioral decisions, the results would have given the appearance of discrepancies between judgment and action. This is because moral judgment level neither discriminated between those deciding to con-tinue or terminate the pregnancy nor between those identifying abor-tion as a moral or a personal issue.

Publication of this book comes at a time when considerable pub-lic debate rages over abortion. Of course, the issue of abortion has been in the public eye for some time now, and will likely remain so for a number of years. However, I believe that Professor Smetana's findings are especially germane to recent events in the U.S. Senate regarding abortion legislation. A subcommittee of the Senate Judiciary Committee has recently held hearings on a bill to declare as federal policy that life begins at conception. The bill is designed to offset a 1973 Supreme Court ruling (Roe v. Wade) that excludes the unborn from the meaning of "person" under the Fourteenth Amendment. Passage of the bill would allow states to declare abortion a crime.

In support of the bill, biologists were brought in to testify that human life begins at conception. However, biologists are seriously divided on what constitutes a meaningful definition of the start of life. It is apparent from the information presented in this book that non-biologists are also divided on a meaningful definition of personhood. Although most participants in this research recognize that life can be said to begin, in a technical-biological sense, at conception, differences of viewpoint stem from philosophical and moral considerations. Participants in the research made it clear that they had ideas regarding the meaning of person, the definition of a life with human rights, and the difficult question of when the unborn can be regarded separately from the mother. Professor Smetana's fine book shows that the Senate subcommittee's exercise, and even passage of the bill, will not go far in quieting the abortion debate.

University of California—Berkeley

ACKNOWLEDGMENTS

As is always the case with an intellectual undertaking such as this, it is enormously difficult to give adequate recognition to all of the people who contributed to the preparation of this book. This book is based on my doctoral dissertation at the University of California at Santa Cruz. I am especially grateful to my thesis committee—Nancy Adler, Brewster Smith, and Elliot Turiel—not only for their advice and encouragement in the preparation of the thesis but also for their unfailing support throughout my graduate career. Each has contributed in a unique way to my thinking and research, and to each I am enormously indebted.

I am also grateful to the research assistants who worked so diligently and with such enthusiasm on various aspects of the research: to Mario Kelly and Karen Letourneau, who coded the adolescent interviews; to Martha Morehouse for her excellent statistical skills and perseverance in conducting the analyses and for her scoring of interviews; and to Doreen Schack for her critical comments in the development of the coding manual and for her tireless energy in recruiting and interviewing the adolescent respondents described in Chapter 6.

I wish to thank Herbert Ginsburg, Nancy Kossan, Karen Letourneau, Anne McMahon, Larry Nucci, Brewster Smith, and Elliot Turiel for their careful reading of the manuscript and for their incisive comments. Thanks are also due to Janice Krinsky, Karen Letourneau, and Deborah Rivkin for patience above and beyond the call of duty in typing and retyping the manuscript.

This research was generously supported by a University of California, Santa Cruz, Patent Fund Grant; a Society for the Psychological Study of Social Issues research award; a National Science Foundation Grant no. BNS76-88384; and a National Institute of Child Health and Human Development Post-Doctoral Fellowship no. 1 F32 HD5618-01.

Finally, I would like to thank the agencies and their staffs for their cooperation and patience. And of course, my heartfelt thanks to the women who shared so much of themselves at what was for many a very difficult point in their lives. Without them, this research would not have been possible.

CONTENTS

LIST OF TABLES AND FIGURE

CONCEPTS OF
SELF AND MORALITY

1

PSYCHOLOGICAL
PERSPECTIVES
ON ABORTION

Few decisions have as potentially a profound effect upon women's
lives as the choice to continue or terminate an unwanted pregnancy.
The choice may be even more difficult when the decision maker is
young, single, and pregnant for the first time. This characterizes
the situation of the women whose reasoning is explored in the following chapters. The decision to continue or terminate an unwanted
pregnancy is discussed, not as an isolated choice but, rather, in relation to the ways that individuals conceptualize—and act upon—the
social world.

Abortion raises a plethora of fundamental questions. These
include, but are not limited to, issues concerning the rights of the
fetus; the meaning, quality, and definition of human life; women's
reproductive rights; women's roles in society; the rights of an individual versus those of society; and sexual mores. Abortion is clearly
a multifaceted and complex issue; an adequate conceptualization of
thinking about this issue must be sensitive to the multiplicity of meanings abortion arouses, not only as a social issue in the public arena
but also in individual women's lives. This book examines individuals'
reasonings about abortion through interviews with women making decisions about unwanted pregnancy and with nonpregnant males and females. Through the analysis of differences in language, sophistica-
tion, and opinion obtained in these interviews, two common themes,
or ways of conceptualizing abortion, emerged. These are referred
to here as moral and personal issues. These labels are derived from
structural–developmental theory (Kohlberg 1969, 1971; Piaget 1970a;
Turiel 1979, forthcoming) and are not meant to be pejorative; rather,
they indicate the continuity between individuals' thinking about abortion and their thinking about other moral and personal issues.

Philosophical treatises and psychological studies of abortion
suggest that although moral and personal issues are complexly inter-

1

woven, they are distinct. At one extreme, conservative Catholic philosophers believe that human life begins at conception, that this life is God-given, and that abortion therefore involves the taking of a human life—a violation of a sacred value (Callahan 1970; Noonan 1970; St. John-Stevas 1963). Traditionally, this viewpoint has favored the life of the child rather than the self-determination of the mother and has been evidenced in resolutions that link the sanctioning of abortion to a more general devaluation of human life. At the other extreme, the fetus is regarded as part of the woman's body rather than a separate life, and arguments for abortion rest on the right of the woman to freely control her body and reproductive life (Callahan 1970; Potter 1969; Szasz 1966; Tangri 1976). While these examples do not do justice to the complexity and diversity of philosophical arguments surrounding abortion, they characterize the moral and personal issues involved.

The contention that the moral and personal concerns of abortion are conceptually distinct is not based exclusively upon the philosophical debate on abortion. Similar distinctions emerge in empirical studies of beliefs and attitudes toward abortion.

PSYCHOLOGICAL RESEARCH ON ABORTION

Given the current interest in abortion, surprisingly little is known about the psychological aspects of unwanted pregnancy and the decision to seek abortion. Psychological research on abortion has explored the relationship between personal attributes, such as personality and attitudes, and the decision to abort or continue an unwanted pregnancy. For example, psychologists have sought to identify the personality characteristics of women who decide to seek abortion compared with those who continue their pregnancies. Early research on this aspect of the abortion experience reflected prevailing conceptions of abortion as a deviant act, or norm violation. Guided by psychoanalytic notions of intrapsychic conflict, researchers attempted to identify the common neurotic or pathological characteristics of women who chose abortion (Ford, Castelnuovo-Tedesco, and Long 1972; Miller 1973; Rapoport 1965; Simon, Senturia, and Rothman 1967). Based on case reports of patients hospitalized for prior mental disturbance, these investigations typically concluded that women who aborted unwanted pregnancies had unconscious motivations toward sadomasochism and disruptions in female role identity (Ford, Castelnuovo-Tedesco, and Long 1972).

These studies were conducted prior to the legalization of abortion. At the time, legal abortions were performed primarily upon women demonstrating psychological problems; some women intentionally exaggerated symptoms to obtain legal abortions. Women who resorted to illegal procedures were generally unavailable for study. Among those who were, guilt over resorting to an illegal procedure was confounded with guilt over seeking an abortion. Based on impressionistic data and compromised by methodological problems, such as poor sampling techniques, the conclusions drawn in these studies cannot be generalized for all women.

In 1973, in the Roe v. Wade opinion, the Supreme Court ruled that the decision to seek abortion is a private decision between a woman and her physician, thus ensuring the availability of abortion as a constitutional right of all women. A dramatic shift in attitudes toward abortion occurred among the general population (Arney and Trescher 1976) and also among the research community (Adler 1979a). Subsequent research on personality correlates of abortion decision making reveals that few personality variables relate to the decision. For instance, abortion patients are no more neurotic than a comparable group of nonpregnant women (Kane and Lachensbuck 1973).

Interest in personality correlates of the decision to abort has recently shifted to interest in such variables as self-image, including feminine self-image, and risk taking. Results from these studies are conflicting, but the general conclusion is that there are few personality characteristics that consistently distinguish women who choose abortion from women who decide to continue their pregnancies. Relationships between traditional concepts of femininity and both decisions—to bear a child (Rosen, Ager, and Martindale 1979) or to terminate a pregnancy (Freeman 1977)—have been observed. Comparisons of successful contraceptors with women whose choose abortion suggest that there is a relationship between perceived self-competence and the choice of abortion (Abernathy 1974); aborters have been found to have lower perceived self-competence than effective contraceptors. However, when women who choose to terminate unwanted conceptions are compared with women who deliver their babies, few differences are found in locus of control, ego resilience (Bracken, Klerman, and Bracken 1978), and perceived self-competence (Rosen, Ager, and Martindale 1979).

Several investigators (Barglow et al. 1968; Fischman 1977; Hatcher 1973) report that adolescents who carry their pregnancies to term have a poorer self-image than those who choose abortion. Some (Barglow et al. 1968; Hatcher 1973) attribute these findings to teenagers' desires to maintain control over their lives, establish their own identity, and bolster their self-image. Others assert that the outcome of unwanted pregnancy depends far more on the psychosocial milieu than personality variables and that women do not choose motherhood as a defensive reaction to low self-esteem (Bracken, Hachamovitch, and Grossman 1974; Olson 1980).

While women who choose to terminate their pregnancies do not seem to differ from other women in personality characteristics, they do appear to hold different attitudes toward abortion, pregnancy, and motherhood. Not surprisingly, women who choose abortion have more favorable attitudes toward abortion than women who carry their pregnancies to term (Evans, Selstad, and Welcher 1976; Goldsmith et al. 1970; Jacobsson et al. 1974; Oskamp, Mindick, and Berger 1974; Osofsky and Osofsky 1972; Steinhoff, Smith, and Diamond 1972; Zellman et al. 1980). Positive attitudes toward abortion are one of a constellation of other social factors, including school performance and desired family size, that are associated with the decision to abort a pregnancy (Evans, Selstad, and Welcher 1976; Fischman 1977; Steinhoff, Smith, and Diamond 1972).

While attitudes are a powerful predictor of decisions to terminate or continue a pregnancy, they do not provide an adequate description of the decision-making process, nor do they indicate the beliefs underlying particular attitudinal responses. Attitudes that appear to be similar may be substantively different. For instance, a rejection of abortion based upon dissatisfaction with the quality of available medical care is qualitatively different from a rejection of abortion based upon the belief that abortion is tantamount to murder, although the expressed attitude is the same. Conversely, a concern with the preservation of women's physical and psychological health can result in either an acceptance or rejection of abortion.

There do appear to be specific beliefs about pregnancy, abortion, childbearing, and motherhood that distinguish women who choose abortion from women who continue unwanted pregnancies. Evidence indicates that moral opposition to abortion is an important factor in decisions to carry an unwanted pregnancy to term. For instance, one investigation reveals that in contrast to women who intend to have an abortion, women who plan to continue unwanted pregnancies are more likely to believe that abortion entails terminating an unborn life, that having an abortion would be emotionally traumatic, and that they would feel guilty (Smetana and Adler 1979, 1980). Other investigators (Bracken, Hachamovitch, and Grossman 1974; Diamond et al. 1973) report that some women continue their pregnancies out of moral opposition to abortion, although they do not specify the content of these moral beliefs.

Other research illustrates that while moral reasoning is an important aspect of women's thinking about abortion, it does not characterize all reasoning about this issue. Among a sample of black, unmarried teenagers who chose to have their babies (Fischman 1977), only one-third of the women reported that they found abortion unacceptable because they viewed it as tantamount to "taking a life" or "destroying their own flesh and blood." Some investigators have assumed that all women consider abortion a moral issue and have attempted to describe women's reasoning according to Kohlberg's model (1969, 1971) of moral development (Belenky and Gilligan 1979; Gilligan 1977; Gilligan and Belenky 1980). However, the results of these studies suggest that not all women consider abortion a moral issue, as reasoning about abortion is not easily categorized in this manner. Another interpretation of these results is that considering all reasoning about abortion within the moral domain provides an incomplete conceptualization of women's thinking about the abortion issue.

Empirical studies of beliefs about abortion indicate that thinking about abortion is diverse and can be characterized by fundamentally different types of beliefs. The arguments presented by ethicists in the philosophical debate over abortion also emerge in empirical studies of women's beliefs about abortion. The findings suggest that while some women consider abortion a moral issue of life, other women consider abortion a personal issue of autonomy, control over one's body, and self-determination. Women's beliefs cluster into components that are either related to beliefs about the fetus as a life and the view that abortion is an act of murder or to concerns about the woman's rights and self-determination, including the belief that choice of abortion is important in maintaining women's self-determination, in controlling reproduction, and in protecting the health, rights, and freedom of women (Beswick 1970; Knutson 1973; Smetana 1979; Smetana and Adler 1979; Werner 1976). These two sets of beliefs appear to be mutually exclusive.

The basis for this distinction appears to be individuals' beliefs about when human life begins. Another study suggests that those who are most opposed to abortion believe that human life begins at conception or during the first trimester and that the right to make life/death decisions is God-given. Those who are most favorable to abortion believe that human life begins at birth or later; that the definition of life depends upon humanistic considerations such as consciousness or awareness; and that parents, society, or the individual have the right to make abortion decisions (Knutson 1973).

In addition, social conventions concerning sexual mores, sex-role behavior, and perceived social norms may be important determinants of the decision to abort or continue a pregnancy. Survey data (Rossi 1967; Schur 1965) indicate that favorable attitudes toward abortion may change when it can be inferred that the intentions of the woman in obtaining an abortion are in violation of her acceptance of motherhood. One author (Schur 1965) contends that negative attitudes toward abortion stem from intentions to limit promiscuity and illegitimacy. Additionally, social norms, as indexed by women's perceptions of significant others' expectations regarding their unwanted pregnancy, exert a significant influence on women's decisions to continue or terminate a pregnancy as well as their response to abortion (Smetana and Adler 1979, 1980; Zellman et al. 1980).

When women's psychological reactions to abortion are conceptually distinguished (Adler 1975), two factors emerge. One factor includes emotions of regret, anxiety, depression, anger, and doubt and appears to reflect the more internally based stress of coping with a sense of loss. The second factor includes emotions of guilt, shame, and disapproval and appears to reflect the reaction to the more external, social meaning of abortion—the social stigma and norm violation—associated with unwanted pregnancy.

Evidence from a variety of sources, then, suggests that abortion is a complex and multifaceted issue and that women's reasoning can be characterized by qualitatively different types of beliefs. Women's judgments about abortion may entail moral issues of life, personal issues of autonomy and self-determination, and conventional considerations of sexuality, sex roles, and normative expectations. While there are indications that these concerns are related to women's resolutions of unwanted pregnancies, they have not been explicitly examined in studies of decision making.

More complex models of pregnancy decision making typically describe the abortion decision in terms of a weighing of advantages and disadvantages of alternate behaviors (Bracken, Klerman, and Bracken 1978; Luker 1974; Smetana and Adler 1979, 1980). For instance, one investigator (Luker 1974) asserts that women consider the costs and benefits associated with contraceptive use and nonuse. She concludes that unwanted pregnancy may result from a rational decision-making process in which assessment of the subjectively perceived costs of contraceptive behavior and the perceived costs of pregnancy create an orientation toward risk taking. Actual nonuse of contraceptives results from an assessment of the subjective probabilities assigned to pregnancy and the costs of terminating a pregnancy should it occur.

According to another model based on similar assumptions (Smetana and Adler 1979, 1980), women weigh their beliefs about significant others' expectations regarding their unwanted pregnancies against their beliefs about the consequences that might result from either having an abortion or having the child. These beliefs produce their attitudes toward abortion, and these, in turn, predict whether or not they will decide to have an abortion.

Do all women in this situation of conflict and choice actually weigh the relative advantages and disadvantages of alternative behaviors? Proponents of rational cost/benefit models such as those described above argue that the rationality implied in these models is "psycho-logical," and that it is the psychologically perceived rather

Than the actual advantages and disadvantages of each alternative that are weighed (Adler 1979b). Others assert that this weighing of costs and benefits provides an inaccurate description of the decision-making process, particularly among younger women.

REASONING IN A DEVELOPMENTAL PERSPECTIVE

Research in social development indicates that there are qualitative differences in the way adolescents reason about the world. Adolescence is characterized by changes that transform the world of the child to the world of an adult (Erikson 1968; Freud 1966; Inhelder and Piaget 1958; Kohlberg and Gilligan 1971). Some contend that these revolutionary changes are the result of transformations in the process of thinking (Inhelder and Piaget 1958; Kagan 1971; Kohlberg and Gilligan 1971; Kolhberg and Kramer 1969). Adolescents do not differ from adults merely in the extent of their social knowledge. Rather, they have qualitatively different ways of representing and interpreting the world, processing information, and constructing solutions to the logical, moral, and personal problems they face. While these changes should influence the way adolescents reason about the problems posed by an unwanted pregnancy, developmental perspectives have rarely been employed in studies of decision making about abortion. This is surprising not only in light of evidence that transformations in thinking occur until well into young adulthood (Kohlberg and Kramer 1969) but also with regard to general concerns about the increase in the incidence of unwanted pregnancy among adolescent and young adult women (Baldwin 1977).

Statistics indicate that increasing numbers of young women over the past decade have faced an unwanted pregnancy. There has been a dramatic rise in the number of unwanted pregnancies among unmarried teenage women. Societal trends toward greater sexual experience at increasingly younger ages (Zelnik and Kantner 1980) have led to an absolute increase in pregnancies among adolescents under the age of 14 and an increase relative to older women among adolescents over the age of 14 (Baldwin 1977). Nearly one million unmarried women under the age of 20 become pregnant in the United States each year. Of these, approximately 550,000 bear their children. Nearly a third (31 percent) of all pregnancies in women under the age of 20 end in abortion (National Center for Health Statistics 1979).

Reflecting the rise in unwanted pregnancies, there has also been a dramatic increase in the number of legal abortions performed. Currently, approximately 1.3 million abortions are performed annually (Guttmacher 1976), making abortion the most commonly performed surgical procedure in the United States.

It is surprising, given these facts, that so little is known about adolescent and young women's reasoning in the situation of conflict and choice regarding unwanted pregnancy. Although abortion has been the subject of much philosophical scrutiny and political debate, scant consideration has been given to women's reasoning as they face the real-life dilemma of unwanted pregnancy. The studies described in this book explore reasoning about abortion among never-pregnant and first-pregnant women, who were interviewed at length about abortion and other issues.

The foregoing discussion also indicates that an adequate description of decision making about abortion should also include a consideration of the qualitative changes in reasoning that occur through the process of development. Further, research requires a conceptual framework to describe the complexity and richness of women's reasoning and the relationship between reasoning and decision making about unwanted pregnancy. As the previous research on abortion reviewed in this chapter illustrates, abortion is a multifaceted issue. Judgments about abortion may entail moral issues of life; social-conventional issues of sexuality and sex role standards; and personal issues of individuality, autonomy, and self-determination. The following chapter describes a conceptual framework of the development of moral, social-conventional, and personal concepts. This model will be employed in the investigations of women's reasoning and decision making about abortion described in this book.

2

DOMAINS OF
SOCIAL-COGNITIVE
DEVELOPMENT

Chapter 1 concluded with the assertion that thinking about abortion is structured by conceptions of self, society, and morality and that reasoning and decision making about abortion should be considered in terms of an individual's understanding of these issues. The research presented in this book is based upon a structural-developmental theory of social development. This constructivist approach, originating from the work of Jean Piaget (1950, 1967, 1970a), describes the origins and development of social knowledge and behavior. According to this theory, moral, social-conventional, and personal concepts are integral but independent aspects of the individual's structuring of the social world.

The central concern of all structural-developmental theories is to describe the acquisition of knowledge and its underlying organization or structure. This differs from other approaches that seek to describe the content of knowledge, or the specific beliefs, attitudes, or facts acquired.

Social development has often been described as the internalization of cultural values or societal standards. According to these models, the child internalizes the standards of its society through the rewards and punishments of socializing agents, such as parents or teachers. While researchers differ as to the acquisition mechanisms posited to account for this process, all internalization models define social development as conformity to cultural norms. For instance, social-learning theorists postulate that imitation, rewards, and punishments shape the child's response, either directly or through delayed cognitive mediation (Aronfreed 1968; Bandura and McDonald 1963; Cheyne 1971; Slaby and Parke 1971). Others (Sears, Maccoby, and Levin 1957; Whiting 1960) posit a more global internalization of social rules. Given these formulations, research then examines the strength, or accuracy, of the internalization by examining the degree of correspondence between the child's behavior and adult standards. This is taken as an indication of the child's development. According to all internalization approaches, behavior is maintained through the imposition of internal or external sanctions.

In contrast, development as discussed herein refers to transformations in the child's thought and action. All structural-developmental theories share several assumptions about the process or form of development (Flavell and Wohlwill 1969; Inhelder and Piaget 1958, 1964; Kohlberg 1971; Piaget 1970a; Werner 1957). First, the process of development is seen as self-constructed and self-regulated. The child actively organizes experience rather than passively incorporating parental norms in his attempts to master the social world. Meaning and social knowledge are thought to arise from the child's continuous interaction with and structuring of the environment.

The developing child's attempts to impose order on social experience results in structures for interpreting the world. These represent neither a copy of parental teachings nor an inaccurate or incomplete copy of the external environment; rather, the child structures the social world, and these structures are constantly changing through social experience. Therefore, development can be described as progress through a sequence of organized structures of thought produced from interactions. These structures are qualitatively transformed through development. Each stage, or way of representing the world, represents a progressive advance over the previous stage.

Finally, it is through the child's efforts to actively organize experience that stage change occurs. Since stage change entails the reorganization of one form of thinking into another, stages progress through an invariant sequence, or order of succession, in development. The understanding acquired at the previous stage is logically necessary for the construction of knowledge at the following stage; stages cannot be skipped, and stages progress in a hierarchical order. Since the stages are successively transformed rather than added on to one another, regression cannot occur. All individuals progress through the same sequence of developmental stages, although they may vary in the rate and extent of development (Kohlberg 1971; Piaget 1970a).

The research described herein is based upon the assumption that knowledge develops within structurally independent domains. Different types of concepts are constructed through the child's active ordering of experience. The social world is diverse, and individuals engage in qualitatively different types of social interactions based upon their experiences with different classes of persons and events. Therefore, the types of knowledge the individual constructs depend in part upon the nature of the environment. Different types of interactions produce different conceptual systems of social knowledge.

Three conceptual domains have been identified as forming the basis of the individual's construction of the social world: the psychological domain, which pertains to knowledge of self, identity, and the causes of one's own and others' behavior; the moral domain, which pertains to concepts of justice and fairness; and the societal domain, which includes issues of social regulation and social organization. A variety of issues may be included within each of these three domains, but each domain is hypothesized to be developmentally and conceptually distinct, parallel, and irreducible to one another. There may be points of intersection, coordination, or overlap between the domains, or they may be coordinated in the sense that one system provides information that stimulates or facilitates change in another. However, they are not viewed as interdependent systems. Thinking is organized and changes sequentially within a domain but not across domains. [1] That is, the unity of organization is taken here to apply only within conceptual domains. The concept of structure does not imply a total unity of mental processes. All aspects of an individual's thinking are not assumed to be interrelated, nor is it assumed that development originates from or proceeds toward such interrelatedness. Thus it is asserted that individuals construct different types of concepts, each of which can be described by a coherence or unity of organization that is distinguishable from each of the other conceptual frameworks. Each domain follows a distinct sequence in development that is characterized by sequential changes in the organization of concepts.

The following sections describe the form and process of development within the moral, social-conventional, and personal domains, respectively. The empirical evidence reviewed in this chapter indicates that moral, social-conventional, and personal concepts are fundamentally distinct, parallel, and irreducible ways of thinking about the social world.

MORAL REASONING

Individuals construct moral concepts, or concepts of justice or fairness, from interactions involving psychological harm or benefit to another, trust, responsibility, and the distribution of resources. Moral considerations arise from factors intrinsic to actions, such as the violation of rights, the harm inflicted upon others, or the effects of the act upon the welfare of others. Awareness of the intrinsic features of the acts results in prescriptive (moral) judgments about how people ought to behave toward others (Turiel forthcoming).

Kohlberg's theory of moral judgment (1969, 1971, 1976) provides one of the most comprehensive models of moral development. According to Kohlberg, moral development progresses through three

TABLE 1

Kohlberg's Definition of Moral Stages

Level 1

At this level the child is responsive to cultural rules and labels of good and bad, right or wrong, but interprets these labels in terms of either the physical or the hedonistic consequences of action (punishment, reward, exchange of favors) or in terms of the physical power of those who enunciate the rules and labels. The level is divided into two stages:

<table>
<tr><td>

Stage 1

The punishment and obedience orientation. The physical consequences of action determine its goodness or badness regardless of the human meaning or value of these consequences. Avoidance of punishment and unquestioning deference to power are valued in their own right, not in terms of respect for an underlying moral order supported by punishment and authority (the latter being stage 4).

</td><td>

Stage 2

The instrumental relativist orientation. Right action consists of that which instrumentally satisfies one's own needs and occasionally the needs of others. Human relations are viewed in terms of those of the marketplace. Elements of fairness, of reciprocity and equal sharing are present, but they are always interpreted in a physical pragmatic way. Reciprocity is a matter of "you scratch my back and I'll scratch yours"—not of loyalty, gratitude, or justice.

</td></tr>
</table>

Level 2

At this level, maintaining the expectations of the individual's family, group, or nation is perceived as valuable in its own right, regardless of immediate and obvious consequences. The attitude is not only one of conformity of personal expectations and social order but of loyalty to it, of actively maintaining, supporting, and justifying the order and of identifying with the persons or group involved in it. At this level, there are two stages:

<table>
<tr><td>

Stage 3

The interpersonal concordance or "good-boy/nice-girl" orientation. Good behavior is that which pleases or helps others and is approved by them. There is much conformity to stereotypical images of what is majority or "natural" behavior.

</td><td>

Stage 4

The "law and order" orientation. There is orientation toward authority, fixed rules, and the maintenance of the social order. Right behavior consists of doing one's duty, showing respect for authority, and maintaining the given social order for its own sake.

</td></tr>
</table>

Level 3

At this level, there is a clear effort to define moral values and principles that have validity and application apart from the authority of the groups or persons holding these principles and apart from the individual's own identification with these groups. This level again has two stages:

<table>
<tr><td>

Stage 5

The social-contract legalistic orientation generally with utilitarian overtones. Right action tends to be defined in terms of general individual rights and in terms of standards that have been critically examined and agreed upon by the whole society. There is a clear awareness of the relativism of personal values and opinions and a corresponding emphasis upon procedural rules for reaching consensus. This is the "official" morality of the United States Constitution.

</td><td>

Stage 6

The universal ethical principle orientation. Right is defined by the decision of conscience in accord with self-chosen ethical principles appealing to logical comprehensiveness, universality, and consistency. These principles are abstract and ethical (the Golden Rule, the categorical imperative); they are not concrete moral rules like the Ten Commandments. At heart, these are universal principles of justice, of the reciprocity and equality of human rights, and of respect for the dignity of human beings as individual persons.

</td></tr>
</table>

levels, encompassing six sequential stages of logically more adequate concepts of justice. These are summarized in Table 1. According to Kohlberg, for the young child morality is external to the self and is oriented toward power, punishment, and physical consequences. At the first stage, which usually occurs at around age seven or eight, morality is defined in terms of power, obedience, and punishment of those who deviate. This stage is often called the punishment and obedience stage, as judgments of right and wrong are determined by the avoidance of punishment and deference to those in authority. These are valued in their own right, rather than representing respect for an underlying moral order.

At the second stage, sometimes called the stage of instrumental relativism or hedonism, the right or good is defined as an equal exchange of favors. At this stage, the goal of reciprocity is to gain an equal share, and the right or good is that which satisfies one's own needs. Elements of fairness or reciprocity appear, but they are interpreted in a physically pragmatic way. The Golden Rule, to treat others as you wish to be treated, is interpreted in a pragmatic way as "you scratch my back and I'll scratch yours."

The moral orientation at the second level, including stages 3 and 4, is toward maintaining or conforming to the rules of society. According to Kohlberg, a stage 3 conception of justice involves stereotypical notions of good and nice behavior; accordingly, this stage is often labeled the "good-boy/nice-girl" stage. The right or good entails a concern for others' approval, mutual affection, and mutual gratitude. At this stage, behavior is frequently judged by intention; "he means well" becomes important for the first time, and approval can be earned by being "nice." Moral judgments are expressed in terms of interpersonal relationships rather than relationships to the wider social order. Thus to be moral—to be fair, right, or good—may be the action that pleases parents, peers, or significant others.

Stage 4, sometimes referred to as law-and-order morality, provides a broader perspective on morality. The sphere of interpersonal relations is transformed to include a consideration of the rules and laws of society. Justice conceptions are no longer derived from the reciprocity or equality between individuals, but rather from relations between the individual and the social system. The right or good is now redefined as adherence to the rules of the social system and involves an orientation toward justice based on maintaining or conforming to the rules of society. While active maintenance of the social order represents a significant advance over the stage 1 orientation toward merely obeying the rules of those in authority, there are limitations to the stage 4 perspective. It provides no mechanism for social change or for the creation of new rules and norms, and it does not recognize those individuals who are outside the social order and wish to change it. Accordingly, the next level provides an orientation toward making rules or laws.

At the highest level, referred to as principled morality, moral judgments are autonomous and based on internal principles, such as the universal principle of justice or reciprocity. Only at this level are moral decisions truly autonomous. Again, this level is divided into two stages. The basis for stage 5 is a justice conception of reciprocity based on social contract. The right or good is that which maximizes the welfare of all. The emphasis is upon individual rights and standards that have been agreed upon by the whole society. The relativism of personal values and opinions is recognized, and there is therefore a corresponding emphasis upon procedural rules for reaching consensus. Aside from what is constitutionally and democratically agreed upon, the "right" is a matter of personal values and opinions. The result is an emphasis upon the "legal point of view," but with an added emphasis upon the possibility of changing a law in terms of rational considerations of social utility (rather than freezing it in terms of stage 4 "law and order"). Outside the legal realm, free agreement and contract are the binding elements of obligation. This is the "official" morality of the U.S. government and Constitution. However, according to Kohlberg, while this stage yields a set of procedural principles on which all individuals could agree, it does not yield a universal morality of obligations and choices.

At stage 6, morality is based upon the principle of justice. The conception of justice is considered universal because moral decisions at this stage are the most just decisions for each individual in the situation, assuming that each individual is considered equal (Rawls 1971). Thus, Kohlberg (1971) states that the stage 6 perspective is not the perspective of the greatest good nor of the ideal spectator, but rather the perspective shared by persons concerned with justice. Right is defined in accordance with self-chosen ethical principles, such as the universal principle of justice. These principles are abstract and ethical—for example, the Golden Rule or the categorical imperative—and appeal to logical comprehensiveness, universality, and consistency. Thus, at stage 6, the dignity of human beings as individual persons is respected and human rights are treated as equal and reciprocal.

Research conducted on Kohlberg's stage formulation provides some support for the model. The same sequence of development has been observed in a variety of cultures, although the rate and extent of development have been observed to vary (Kohlberg 1969, 1971). Research evidence also supports the basic claim of the invariance of the sequence in development (Colby, Kohlberg, and Gibbs 1979; Turiel 1966) and indicates that while children prefer moral reasoning at a higher level than their own, they do not adequately comprehend reasoning structured at more than one level above their own (Rest, Turiel, and Kohlberg 1969).

Recently, the validity of the final two stages of moral judgment described by Kohlberg has been challenged by adherents of the theory (Gibbs 1977, 1979), who question whether these stages meet the Piagetian criteria for sequential stages. On the basis of longitudinal evidence, Kohlberg and his colleagues (Colby, Kohlberg, and Gibbs 1979) have modified the scheme to exclude stage 6. They acknowledge that the rarity of this stage in their (and other) studies casts doubt upon its validity as a universal stage of development.

Nevertheless, according to this global notion of moral development, all social reasoning would be considered within the moral domain. Thus, according to Kohlberg, all reasoning about abortion (or other social issues) could be classified according to this scheme.

SOCIAL-CONVENTIONAL REASONING

More serious criticisms of Kohlberg's model have been raised by another researcher (Turiel 1975, 1978a, 1978b, 1979, forthcoming), who claims that the moral domain has been defined too broadly. In Kohlberg's scheme, as well as in other models of moral development (Piaget 1948), reasoning about morality and reasoning about other aspects of social systems have been confused. In Kohlberg's scheme, autonomous morality is viewed as emerging through its differentiation from other normative aspects of social systems. No distinction is made between rules that are arbitrary and relative to the social context and the more prescriptive and universal moral rules. Thus, not until late adolescence when principled reasoning emerges would adolescents be expected to distinguish between rules pertaining to justice and welfare and rules that primarily serve to regulate social order.

Turiel claims that individuals at all ages construct an understanding of social organization and social convention that is distinct from concepts of justice. He maintains that thinking about society and social systems is an independent aspect of the developing child's thought. According to this view, morality must be more narrowly defined as justice and must be distinguished from concepts of social organization.

Social conventions are defined as the behavioral uniformities that serve to coordinate social interaction and maintain social systems. They are generated through an understanding of the regularities in the environment, such as regularities in forms of address, manners, dress, and sex roles. Unlike moral events, social-conventional events are not in themselves intrinsically prescriptive; they are consensually determined uniformities that coordinate inter- actions within social systems. They are arbitrary and relative to the social context in that other actions could serve the same function. Acts of this type are referred to as within the societal domain because they are structured by concepts of social organization. It has been hypothesized that concepts of society and social convention form a system of social knowledge separate from morality that is structured by underlying concepts of social organization (Turiel 1975, 1978b, 1979, forthcoming).

Evidence from both cross-sectional and longitudinal studies in- dicates that concepts within this domain are successively transformed through development (Turiel 1975, 1979, in preparation). Social- conventional concepts undergo age-related changes that entail suc- cessive oscillations between affirmation and negation of the impor- tance of social conventions in structuring social interactions and maintaining social life; these levels are summarized in Table 2. Children develop an increasing understanding of the regulative func- tion of social conventions in maintaining social groups and in struc- turing social interaction. At the earliest level, occurring at approx- imately age six or seven, social uniformities are observed, but they are not understood as ways of coordinating social interactions; rather, they are assumed to be descriptive of the social world and therefore necessary. For instance, children at this level assert that occupa- tions, such as doctor or nurse, are necessarily associated with gen- der.

At the second level, children attend to the arbitrariness of con- vention. While children understand that empirical uniformities exist in behavior, uniformity does not imply necessity. For instance, the association of roles, labels, and activities with classes of people is no longer seen as necessary. Since the acts are regarded as arbi- trary, children reject the necessity of adhering to convention.

Not until the third level, occurring at around age 10 or 11, are social conventions related to elementary notions of the social system. At this level, concrete concepts of social systems emerge. Three elements of social structure—authority, adherence to rules, and maintenance of social order—are now related to convention. Social relationships are now seen as governed by a system in which individ- uals hold positions of authority, such as teacher or principal. Al- though conventions, such as the assertion that doctors are men and nurses are women, are regarded as arbitrary, children at this level believe they should be followed. The expectations of authority are seen to vary from one context to another, but they require obedience.

At the fourth level, conventions are regarded as nothing but the expectations of others, and therefore adherence to them is again con-

TABLE 2

Major Changes in Social-Conventional Concepts

Level	Summary of Social-Conventional Concepts
1	Convention as descriptive of social uniformity. Convention is viewed as descriptive of uniformities in behavior and is not conceived as part of the structure or function of social interaction. Conventional uniformities are descriptive of what is assumed to exist. Conventions are maintained to avoid violation of empirical uniformities.
2	Negation of convention as descriptive of social uniformity. Empirical uniformity is not a sufficient basis for maintaining conventions. Conventional acts are regarded as arbitrary, and conventions are not conceived as part of structure or function of social interaction.
3	Convention as affirmation of rule system; early concrete conception of social system. Convention is now seen as arbitrary and changeable. Adherence to convention is based on concrete rules and authoritative expectations, and conceptions of conventional acts are not coordinated with conceptions of rule.
4	Negation of convention as part of rule system. Conventions are now seen as arbitrary and changeable regardless of rules. An evaluation of rules pertaining to conventional acts is coordinated with evaluations of the act itself. Conventions are seen as "nothing but" social expectations.
5	Convention as mediated by social system. At this stage there is the emergence of systematic concepts of social structure. Convention is seen as normative regulation in a system with uniformity, fixed roles, and a static hierarchical organization.
6	Negation of convention as societal standards. Conventions are regarded as codified societal standards. Uniformity in convention is not considered to serve the function of maintaining social systems. Conventions are "nothing but" societal standards that exist through habitual use.
7	Convention as coordination of social interactions. Conventions are viewed as uniformities that are functional in coordinating social interactions. Shared knowledge, in the form of conventions, among members of social groups is seen to facilitate interaction and the operation of the system.

sidered unnecessary. The acts are viewed as arbitrary, and therefore social expectations are rejected as an insufficient basis for prescribing behavior.

The fifth level, occurring at midadolescence, marks the emergence of systematic concepts of social structure. Social conventions are regarded as normative regulations in a system with fixed roles, uniformity, and static, hierarchical organization. Conventions are seen to regulate relations between individuals that are determined by social organization. That is, conventions symbolize both roles and status. For instance, relationships between teacher and student are determined by the school context and hierarchical social roles. Inequities in status must be signified by conventional usages, such as proper forms of address.

The next level involves the negation of convention as "nothing but" societal standards that exist through habitual use. The negation of convention at this level represents a rejection of the reasoning at the previous level. Conventions are still viewed as part of the social system, but uniformity per se is no longer regarded as a necessary condition for the adequate functioning of the social system. Therefore, conventions are regarded as unduly arbitrary and diversity in behavior is seen as compatible with social organization. Uniformities in convention (now regarded as codified societal standards) are not seen as serving the function of maintaining the social system.

Not until the highest level, achieved in young adulthood, are social conventions regarded as agreed-upon regularities. They are regarded as serving the function of coordinating interactions between individuals in social systems. Social-conventional uniformities are therefore seen as increasingly necessary in the coordination of social interactions.

The understanding of convention stems from individuals' conceptions of social systems. Development within the societal domain reflects a continuous dialectical process of affirmation and negation of the importance of convention in maintaining social interactions. The negation phase, which entails a reevaluation of the conception of social structure developed at the previous stage, appears to be necessary for each new construction of conceptions of social structure.

Thus, according to this research, social-conventional issues such as sex roles and sexual mores must be distinguished from moral judgments in women's thinking about abortion. The research discussed in this book is consistent with this approach. That is, morality is narrowly defined as justice pertaining to a limited range of issues, such as the value of life, harm, trust, responsibility, and the fair distribution of resources, and is treated as distinct from concepts of social convention.

Social conventions must also be distinguished from conceptions of self and personal issues. The psychological domain has been defined as individuals' psychological understandings of their own and others' behaviors. This includes social inferences about others' thoughts, feelings, motives, and intentions (these studies have been extensively reviewed by Shantz 1975), as well'as individuals' conceptions of self and identity. Research on conceptions of self and personal issues, hypothesized to be one aspect of the psychological domain, are discussed below.

PERSONAL REASONING

Nucci (1977, 1981) hypothesizes that control over personal issues is central to the establishment of the "self" in society. Societies may define their control over individuals more extensively than individuals may prefer. By considering an action, event, or issue as a personal matter, the individual places that event under his or her own authority. Personal reasoning is organized around concepts of the actor as an autonomous individual and issues related to the maintenance of the self. This includes the set of behaviors that are perceived by individuals to pertain only to themselves and that are of minor consequence to others. The personal domain is defined by actions perceived by the individual to be outside the realm of societal regulation and moral concern. Personal thought may develop from actions or events involving intrusions of privacy, respect for individuality, and control over one's physical state. Research on personal actions has included judgments about the choice of one's friends, the content of one's private communications, and control over one's body, including physical appearance and masturbation (Nucci 1977, 1981).

Empirical evidence suggests that an individual's thinking about personal issues follows a developmental sequence closely associated with the individual's understanding of the self. Through development, an understanding of the self as a concrete, physical entity is gradually transformed to more labile concepts of self as a process or personality construct. These personal concepts are summarized in Table 3. In the earliest level, found among children approximately seven to eight years old, the self is viewed as one's physical body, and personal actions are viewed concretely as the area owned by the individual and subject to personal control. Personal issues, such as privacy or control over one's appearance, are all described in terms of ownership. For instance, children at this stage might claim that their privacy (or their hair) belongs to them, and that therefore they should be able to do as they please. Control over personal issues is used to establish concrete distinctions between self and other.

At the second level, occurring around age 10, children define the self by their body, activities, and characteristic role relations. Distinctions between self and other now become differentiated and

TABLE 3

Major Changes in Personal Concepts

Level	Summary of Personal Concepts
1	Personal domain as possession; personal concerns focus upon concrete distinctions between the self and others. The concrete nature of level 1 conceptions of the personal is consistent with the definition of self as the physical body and the equation of individual identity with unique aspects of appearance. At this level the personal domain is objectified and treated as a material possession, thereby justifying self-regulation of personal matters. The importance of personal regulation is that it permits the establishment and maintenance of a set of concrete distinctions between the self and the group. Regulation of one's activities and private affairs serves to foster and maintain a sense of uniqueness, self-mastery, and competence.
2	Personal concerns focus upon the development of a personal style, the attainment of positive social status, and the avoidance of embarrassment. At this level conceptions of the person shift to a definition of self that includes the notion of personality defined as a set of characteristic behaviors. Coincident with this change, the view of the group as mere "other" shifts to an awareness of the group as evaluator of individual personal qualities. Autoregulation of one's personal affairs permits the person to engage in public activities that express and develop the personality while also garnishing a positive social label. Personal regulation of one's private affairs permits the person to keep hidden from public view those personal activities or characteristics that might lead to public ridicule, embarrassment, or misunderstanding.
3	Personal concerns center on the maintenance of the individual defined as a set of thoughts, feelings, or opinions that differ from those of others. This level marks the shift from reasoning about the person in terms of external visible characteristics to a conception of the person in terms of internal cognitive processes. At level 3 the person is equated with an individual set of thoughts, values, and so forth, that differ from those of others. It is through the exercise of choice regarding personal matters that one maintains individuality.
4	Central concern entails the coordination of all aspects of personal experience into an internally consistent self system. At this point control over personal affairs is viewed as essential to the coordination of all aspects of the self into an internally consistent whole. The core of this personal system is an essence that is the inner "true self." Regulation of one's personal affairs permits the individual to come to know and understand the self and develop the self's potential.
5	Central concerns focus on personal decisions serving to create and transform the labile self. The conception of an inner "true self" as the core of personal life has been replaced by the process of personal decision making based upon a subjective assessment of the course of action that will lead to personal happiness. Self is no longer seen as a coordinated system but rather a construct used to refer to the sum of all personal experience. Autoregulation of one's personal affairs is essential if the creation of self is to follow the individual's subjectively valued course.

20

entail notions of individual differences based on behavioral characteristics. Children distinguish themselves from other children in terms
of behaviors or activities; they also emphasize qualitative distinctions
among people. This results in the emergence of a concern with protecting the self from negative social judgments that lead to embarrassment or ridicule. Control over personal matters therefore entails a more complex task of establishing a personal style while protecting the self from embarrassment. This level of development
coincides with the self-consciousness that has been attributed to
early adolescence (Elkind 1967).

The central concern at the third level, typically achieved in the
early teens, is the development and maintenance of individuality, defined reactively as a set of ideas of volitions that differ from those of
others. At this level, notions of self become more psychologically
rather than behaviorally oriented. Self is defined for the first time in
terms of one's thinking rather than one's behaviors. Children assert
that individuality is maintained through the exercise of control over
personal matters. At this level, loss of control over personal matters
entails the risk of absorption by the group by losing all of one's distinguishing psychological features.

At the fourth level, concepts of self, typically achieved in late
adolescence, entail the notion of the self as a coordinated whole—
composed of a "true self" or essence, and an outer, public self or
persona. Personal actions are viewed as necesssary to both the
maintenance of the true self and the presentation of the public self.
Thus, control over personal affairs is now seen as essential to the
coordination of all aspects of self into an internally consistent whole.
Individuals assert that they come to know and understand the self,
behave in a manner that is consistent with the self, and grow and develop through self-regulation of personal matters.

Notions of self as a stable essence are transformed to a more
transcendent notion of self in the final level, achieved in later adolescence. At this level, the self is viewed as a construct, a temporal,
evolving product of one's decisions; thus, making personal decisions
becomes the process by which the self is created and transformed.

The same age-related changes in descriptions of self from concrete, external physical characteristics to an internal, psychological
self have been documented in several studies pertaining to conceptions
of self, emotions, and descriptions of other persons (Broughton 1975,
1978; Gordon 1976; Nucci 1977, 1981; Peevers and Secord 1973; Pratt
1975; Wolfson 1972). These studies suggest that notions of self and
psychological concepts form a unified domain of thought. The remainder of this book will refer to personal issues rather than to the
psychological domain to limit the discussion to personal issues. However, it should be noted that they are hypothesized to be structurally
related to other aspects of the psychological domain.

DOMAIN DISTINCTIONS AND CONFUSIONS

The evidence just reviewed indicates that moral and social-conventional concepts follow distinct, sequential courses of development. Empirical evidence suggests that children at all ages consistently distinguish between these different types of events and that bases upon which these distinctions are made are constant across the ages studied. For instance, research examining distinctions between social conventions and morality indicates that children of all ages consistently consider moral transgressions more serious offenses than social-conventional transgressions and moral rules more important than conventional rules (Damon 1977; Nucci 1981; Smetana 1981; Smetana, Bridgeman, and Turiel forthcoming; Turiel 1978a). Moreover, conventional events are evaluated as relative to the social context and contingent upon the presence of rules while moral events are not (Smetana 1981; Turiel 1978a; Weston and Turiel 1980). In addition, evaluations of moral events are based upon their intrinsic harmful or unjust consequences for others, while social-conventional events are evaluated on the basis of their regulation of the social order and normative expectation (Nucci 1981; Nucci and Nucci in press; Smetana 1980).

Empirical evidence also suggests that these different concepts develop out of different social interactions. The results of several observational studies of naturally-occurring moral and social-conventional events indicate that different types of social interactions are associated with different types of events. For instance, preschool children spontaneously initiate responses to moral transgressions that consist of statements concerning the harm inflicted upon the victim (Much and Schweder 1978; Nucci and Turiel 1978). These responses are in contrast to the observed responses to conventional violations. Teachers, but not preschool children, respond to conventional transgressions with statements concerning the prohibitions regarding the acts or the effects of the act upon the social order. With increasing age, children initiate responses to social-conventional events that focus upon the rules prohibiting such acts or the act's social regulatory function (Nucci and Nucci in press).

Support for the distinctions between domains also comes from studies wherein the domains have been confused. Kohlberg's scheme of moral development has been applied to a wide range of behaviors and actions. These have included reasoning about civil rights (Haan, Smith, and Block 1968), capital punishment (Kohlberg and Elfenbein 1975), interpersonal relationships, sexuality (Gilligan et al. 1971), and abortion (Belenky and Gilligan 1979; Gilligan 1977; Gilligan and Belenky 1980). It cannot be presumed that all of these are necessarily moral concerns for all respondents. Discrepancies observed in the findings of some of these studies may be accounted for by the claim that moral and nonmoral domains have been confused.

For example, in one study, high school students' responses to hypothetical dilemmas about sexuality were scored as moral issues (Gilligan et al. 1971). Moral maturity scores on standardized hypothetical dilemmas were mostly at stage 4, while almost 50 percent of the sample engaged in a lower level of reasoning about the sexual dilemmas than about the other moral dilemmas. Most of these responses consisted of stage 2, instrumentally relative, responses from otherwise stage 4 subjects. This increase in instrumental responses could indicate the occurrence of decalage in the moral domain—that is, within a given stage, development regarding different issues could occur at different rates. It is also possible that personal responses were incorrectly interpreted as stage 2, since reasoning about the self and the importance of an action to the person (the personal domain) most closely resembles a stage 2 response. Further evidence supporting this position comes from a longitudinal follow-up study of the same subjects (Stein 1973). While moral reasoning, as measured by the standard dilemmas, had progressed, reasoning about the sexual dilemmas remained at stage 2.

Similarly, in recent research on abortion, one investigator has assumed that all reasoning about abortion is within the moral domain (Gilligan 1977) and has applied Kohlberg's scheme of moral judgment to the abortion responses. When the scheme did not adequately characterize the observed responses, Gilligan reconstructed Kohlberg's scheme to reflect what she considered to be the separate course of moral development in women—one that reflected women's greater interpersonal concerns. However, this may be an artifact of using abortion to generate the scheme rather than an accurate reflection of interpersonal concerns in the moral domain because, according to structural-developmental theory, the processes of assimilation and accommodation through which development proceeds (Piaget 1970a) should not differ for men and women.

In a further study (Belenky and Gilligan 1979; Gilligan and Belenky 1980), women were reinterviewed to determine the impact of the resolution of the abortion dilemma on reasoning and adjustment. Since stages are transformed in development, it is commonly assumed that regression cannot occur. However, regression in moral reasoning about abortion was reported in over 20 percent of the cases over the one-year period, while no regression was observed in women's judgments about hypothetical moral judgment dilemmas.

It is likely that the conclusions drawn from these studies stem from a confusion between domains and an overgeneralization of the moral domain to nonmoral stimuli. What have often been assumed to be moral stimuli were not necessarily judged to be moral by respondents. In particular, the research on abortion and sexuality suggests that the instrumental relativism of stage 2 moral reasoning has been confused with the general characteristics of personal thought. While reasoning about personal issues—concern over maintaining and establishing the self, and regulation of personal matters—most closely resembles a stage 2 moral response, the former is structured by concepts of self while the latter is structured by concepts of justice. An accurate description of thinking about such issues should entail careful distinctions of the concerns pertaining to these different domains.

The research on social development reviewed in this chapter indicates that moral, social-conventional, and personal concepts are fundamentally distinct, parallel, and irreducible ways of thinking about the social world. Although they are complexly interwoven in judgments about abortion, they should be conceptually and empirically distinguished. Abortion may be considered a moral issue of life, a social-conventional issue of sex roles or sexual mores, or a personal issue of autonomy and individuality. The research reported in the following chapter examines women's reasoning about the moral, social-conventional, and personal issues of abortion in the naturally occurring context of an unwanted pregnancy.

NOTE

1. This view differs from other structural-developmental theories of social development. Others (Keasey 1975; Kohlberg 1969; Kuhn et al. 1977; Selman 1976) have interpreted structural development to mean that all forms of thought are interrelated. These global interpretations of cognitive organization have defined the concept of structure in terms of the unity of all mental processes. For instance, it has been hypothesized that logical, physical, and social concepts are interrelated. In these formulations the stages of cognitive development described by Piaget (1970a) are considered the central cognitive structure upon which the development of social concepts depends. Thus, in one formulation, the development of logical-mathematical thought is seen as necessary but not sufficient for the development of corresponding levels of moral judgment (Kohlberg 1969, 1971; Kuhn et al. 1977).

However, evidence provided in support of the proposed structural interrelatedness has come from correlational studies. This provides an inadequate method of assessing the nature of relationships between different domains of structural development, as such studies can assess only the degree of correspondence in the rate of change of the measures used. Two structurally unrelated aspects of conceptual development could produce a high correlation coefficient if there are systematic relationships in their rates of development. However, this type of evidence does not provide sufficient evidence for their interdependence.

3

MODES OF
REASONING
ABOUT ABORTION

The theory and research described in the previous chapter provides a comprehensive framework for considering women's thinking about the moral, social-conventional, and personal issues of abortion. In the study to be described in this chapter, women facing the real-life dilemma of an unwanted pregnancy were interviewed at length about abortion and other issues. The women, who came from a small coastal town in California, ranged in age from 13 to 32 and were facing first, unwanted pregnancies. Single, never-pregnant women were also interviewed about abortion to provide a comparison with women's reasoning in a situation of conflict and choice.

Pregnant women were interviewed shortly after learning of their unwanted pregnancies and while in the process of decision making. The two-hour interviews were semistructured and designed to elicit women's thinking about the moral, social-conventional, and personal issues of abortion. The interviews were scored for both domain, or type of reasoning, and developmental level of reasoning. This chapter considers women's thinking about the general permissibility of abortion as well as the concerns that structured their decision making. Relationships between reasoning and decision making about unwanted pregnancy and between real-life reasoning and hypothetical moral judgments are considered in Chapter 4.

The following section describes the study design, methods for sample selection, and measures in greater detail. This is followed by qualitative descriptions of reasoning about abortion. The final section presents a task involving the classification of hypothetical issues and statistical analyses of reasoning.

RESEARCH PROCEDURES

A total of 70 single women ranging in age from 13 to 32[1] were referred to the study when they came to one of the five family-planning agencies in a small coastal town in California for a pregnancy test. These agencies represented a spectrum of political and social orientations, from an agency espousing a "pro-life" perspective to a feminist health collective. Counselors at these agencies invited women to participate in the study after informing them of the results of their pregnancy test.

Of the 70 women, 48 were referred when they were informed of their first, unwanted pregnancies. They were interviewed within a week of confirmation of their pregnancies. While the "unwantedness" of a pregnancy is a fluid concept, which may vary throughout pregnancy, all of the participating pregnant women were experiencing unplanned and initially unwanted pregnancies. Of these 48 women, 25 ultimately decided to have an abortion; 23 decided to continue their pregnancies. To compare reasoning between pregnant and nonpregnant women, 22 never-pregnant women equivalent in age to the pregnant women were recruited from the same family-planning agencies and also interviewed about abortion.[2]

Women who chose abortion were similar to women who chose to continue their pregnancies in age, socioeconomic status, religious background, marital status, and current living arrangements—that is, living or not living with their boyfriends. Characteristically they were Caucasian, had never been married, and came from primarily lower middle-class families. They ranged in age from 13 to 32, and were, on the average, 20.78 years old. Over one-third were between the ages of 13 and 18, another third were between the ages of 19 and 22, and the remainder were between the ages of 23 and 32. Their religious backgrounds were diverse, but a high proportion (35 percent) were Catholic.

Women deciding to have an abortion were more educated than women choosing to continue their pregnancies. Women who decided to have an abortion were more likely to be college students or to have completed some postsecondary education; women who chose to continue their pregnancies were typically high-school students or high-school graduates. These differences were also reflected in their mothers' educational levels; mothers of women choosing abortion were more likely to have attended college than mothers of women choosing to continue their pregnancies. Further, while they were in general not very religious, as reflected by church attendance, women who decided to continue their pregnancies were more religious than other women. They reported that they attended church approximately once a month. Women who decided to abort their pregnancies reported that, on the average, they rarely attended church. Women who were continuing their pregnancies were also further along in their pregnancies when they were interviewed than women deciding to have abortions, but most were within the first trimester of their pregnancies. A summary of the demographic characteristics of the study sample is presented in Appendix A.

The theory and research discussed in the previous chapter provided the conceptual basis for the analysis of reasoning. Women's reasoning about abortion was explored using the semistructured clinical interview method of Piaget (1960). This method was designed to assess the underlying organization of thinking rather than particular conclusions or attitudes held. The purpose of the interview was to have the respondent explain her reasoning as fully as possible. Therefore, the information obtained had to be appropriate to an analysis of the structure of thought. While standardized questions were employed, an integral part of such interviews was the elaboration of responses prompted by the interviewer's probing. The interviewer was an active participant in the interview, continually asking the respondent to clarify and expand upon responses. This approach differed from other methods designed to arrive at a quantitative score or conclusion, and from more experimental methods that attempt to reduce bias by controlling all factors in the situation that might affect responses. Rather, underlying reasoning was elicited through extensive probing of responses. Because the respondent was viewed as actively constructing social knowledge, the choices of words and questions asked had to be flexible enough to actively engage and pursue directions of importance to the individual being interviewed.

The goal of the interview was to obtain a full elaboration of each woman's reasoning in the three conceptual domains and the organization of judgments within each domain. At the outset of the interview, women were asked to state their opinions regarding the general permissibility of abortion, including the circumstances and time periods, if any, during which they thought abortion was acceptable. This initial opinion did not, in itself, indicate social-cognitive domain but provided a basis for subsequent assessment of reasoning. The approximately 90-minute interview consisted of semistandardized questions (see Appendix B) regarding the hypothesized moral, social-conventional, and personal issues of abortion. During the initial portion of the interview, women were asked whether they believed abortion to be right or wrong and the basis for this judgment. The moral issues—whether they considered abortion taking a human life and the justifications for such an act—and the personal issues—the importance to women of controlling their bodies and of making personal decisions —were both extensively probed, as were social conventions regarding sexuality, illegitimacy, and the importance of traditional sex roles for women. The women were also asked when they believed the fetus became a human life and the criteria they employed in making such a judgment. Finally, they were questioned about the appropriate role of significant others, such as their parents, partners, and the law, in abortion decision making.

Questions regarding the general permissibility of abortion were followed by a discussion of decision making regarding their own unwanted pregnancies. Women were asked to describe the factors influential in their decisions and the importance of each of the considerations discussed earlier in the interview. Thus, they were asked to make prescriptive judgments about the right and wrong of abortion as well as to describe their own decision making. The same set of issues was pursued in each interview, but issues of importance to a particular respondent were clarified and expanded through probing of responses.

Piaget (1960) had advocated that countersuggestion be employed to assess the firmness with which respondents hold to their own convictions in the face of contrary evidence or opinion. This technique was extremely useful in verifying the steadfastness with which respondents constructed an issue within a domain. Quite strikingly, when presented with issues or reasoning characteristic of a domain different than their own, respondents reformulated the concerns in a domain-appropriate manner or rejected such issues as unimportant or invalid. For instance, when personal reasoners were confronted with moral reasoners' contention that abortion involves taking a life, they asserted that the fetus does not become a life until birth. Similarly, some moral reasoners rejected as unimportant the personal argument that abortion is an issue of personal choice and maintained that abortion entails the issue of life. The use of countersuggestion through the presentation of reasoning in a different domain thus permitted ongoing hypothesis testing during the course of the interview regarding the domain that appropriately characterized the respondent's reasoning about abortion.

In addition, each respondent's level of moral judgment was assessed independently employing two standardized moral judgment dilemmas (Kohlberg et al. 1976).[3] (See Appendix B.)

Half of the interview protocols were employed in the development of a scoring manual, which was they applied to the remainder of the protocols. The scoring manual became the criterion for the raters' scoring of reasoning. Employing descriptions contained in the manual, the rater assigned each respondent's reasoning to one of four mutually exclusive categories indicating either a domain or type of coordination between domains. The rater thus determined the "best fit" for each protocol; one score was derived for the entire protocol.[4] Interjudge agreement between two trained raters on the scoring of 50 percent of the protocols was 88 percent.

QUALITATIVE DESCRIPTIONS OF
REASONING ABOUT ABORTION

Four distinctions emerged from the domain analysis of women's
reasoning about abortion. These distinctions were based upon fundamental differences in the definition of human life. While all women
clearly considered the child a human life at birth, they varied in their
judgments about when the fetus should be considered an independent
or equal human life. This distinguished their conceptualization of
abortion. Women who treated abortion as a moral issue, referred
to here as moral reasoners, considered the fetus a life at conception;
their reasoning about abortion was structured by the issue of life regarding the justifications or lack of justifications for taking life.
Women who treated abortion as a personal issue, referred to here as
personal reasoners, considered the fetus a truly independent life at
birth and, therefore, abortion decisions were viewed as personal decisions. Personal reasoning about abortion was structured by concepts
of the self regarding issues of personal control and self-maintenance.
Women who coordinated personal and moral concerns, referred to
here as coordinated reasoners, were characterized as granting the
fetus human status midway during the pregnancy. While abortion was
considered a personal issue until this point, it was treated as a moral
issue of life once the fetus was regarded as a human life. Finally,
for some, judgments about abortion were marked by conflict, vacillation, or confusion; this type of reasoning will be referred to as uncoordinated, as it illustrated a lack of coordination between issues
in the personal and moral domains. Uncoordinated responses were
characterized by greater variability regarding the definition of life.

Social-conventional issues will not be discussed here, as these
issues were unimportant among women in this sample and were never
raised spontaneously by respondents. They will be discussed further
in Chapter 6.

The following sections elaborate upon the characteristics of
moral, personal, coordinated, and uncoordinated reasoning about
abortion through discussion and examples from the interviews.

Moral Reasoning about Abortion

Of the respondents in this sample, 25 percent treated abortion
as a moral issue. These women considered the unborn child a human
life from conception on; their reasoning about abortion was structured by a concern with justice regarding the issue of life. Characteristically, women who treated abortion as a moral issue defined
human life in terms of its genetic or spiritual potentiality—that is,

because the embryo is genetically or spiritually complete at the moment of conception it must be considered a human life in the abortion decision. While the issue of life was the preeminent concern of all moral reasoners, there was considerable variation in the value ascribed to life. This variation is discussed below according to Kohlberg's scheme of moral development.

The modal stage of moral reasoning about abortion was stage 3, and responses ranged from stage 1 to stage 5. Of the respondents who treated abortion as a moral issue, 29 percent were at stage 1, 18 percent were at stage 2, 24 percent were at stage 3, 12 percent were at stage 4, and 18 percent were at stage 5. The reader should bear in mind that the actual number of respondents at each stage was quite small and that the examples below do not illustrate the full range of reasoning potentially articulated at each developmental stage.

Stage 1 Moral Reasoning

For stage 1 moral reasoners, the mere fact of the unborn life's physical existence inside the mother at conception imbues that life with value equal to other (born) human lives. While the fetus's existence within the mother is sufficient to regard it as valuable, the moral value of life is not differentiated from its physical or social value. These reasoners are concrete and literal in their interpretation of abortion as an act of killing. They reason that one should not kill, but they express no moral obligation toward preserving life. Further probing regarding the value of life reveals that they make little distinction between human and animal life; they compare abortion with killing a favored pet. Abortion is regarded as stupid or a difficult thing to do, but there is no moral injunction against killing. Nor do women at this stage evaluate individual motivations or intentions in abortion decisions.

For the most part, stage 1 reasoners reject abortion as a viable alternative for themselves. Their orientation toward the consequences of the act rather than the intentions involved also results in a more general condemnation of abortion. However, they see no reason why, if a woman so chooses, abortion would be wrong. As 17-year-old Karen so vividly expressed it, "it's her bag, her trip."

When asked about the legality of abortion, these women find it difficult to differentiate between laws regarding abortion and laws prohibiting murder. However, they do not find the current legal availability of abortion morally objectionable. This is illustrated in the following two examples.

> A. Yeah, I think the baby is a human being as soon as the seed is in the ovary. It's just knowing that there's

something in there growing. You know it's going to
be born, you know there's going to be somebody there,
and you know that baby's going to grow up to be a
human being someday. I mean it's just like killing a
life, there's no excuse for not having the baby and
killing the poor thing. It wasn't the baby's fault, it
was out of her stupidity. Like mine. Mine was stupid, too, not taking birth control, but as soon as I
got pregnant—you know, I'm taking the responsibility.

Q. Do you think it is the same as killing another person?

A. I do. I really do. I feel strongly about abortions.

Q. Well, whose right do you think it is to make decisions
about abortion?

A. I think it should be up to the person, the girl herself.
If that girl's got a good reason, then it's her reason.
It's up to her. I can't see anybody taking a life of the
baby, but at the same time, I think every girl has the
right to her own opinion, to her own feelings about
it, and if she wants an abortion, it's her bag, it's
her trip.

Q. Well, we make laws telling people you can't kill,
that murder is wrong, and that kind of thing isn't
up to the individual to decide for themselves. Why
is abortion different?

A. There's not really much difference to it. I guess
it's just that I know there's a lot of girls out there
that are for abortion. I hardly know anybody that's
for murder. [Karen, age 17]

Q. So, do you think abortion should be permitted?

A. No! "Cause it's just like killing somebody. That's
why I don't think it should be. Because then it starts
growing and being your insides and stuff. And it
breathes and stuff. In the beginning it also has a
heartbeat so it must still be living. In the fifth and
sixth month, the baby just starts getting all its fin-
gernails and stuff. If you were inside someone's
stomach, would you like to be killed?

Q. So, do you think that all through a pregnancy, it's
like killing another life?

A. Yeah, without giving it a chance to come into the world.

Q. Why do you think it's wrong?

A. Because it's just murdering. I wouldn't kill nobody.

Q. Some women think that it [abortion] should be a woman's right, because it's her body. Do you agree with that?

A. Well, it'll be over in nine months, if they didn't want it, they could get it adopted.

Q. Do you think that's fair to the woman?

A. Yeah.

Q. How come?

A. Because her mother didn't kill her.

Q. What if it is what somebody wants to do? Would that be OK?

A. Well, why would they want to kill a baby? It's stupid. They should just go ahead and have it. And if they didn't want it, even before they were pregnant they could just already find some parents that would want it. And when they have it, they wouldn't have to see it, in case they want it. It's their own fault if they get pregnant anyway. They shouldn't mess around if they didn't expect to have kids. [Kelly, age 13]

Stage 2 Moral Reasoning

Stage 2 moral reasoning embodies some of the concerns articulated at the previous stage, but also entails an advance over the previous mode of thought. For the first time, conflicting perspectives are considered, and early notions of reciprocity are evident. In the above example, rudimentary conceptions of reciprocity emerge in Kelly's rhetorical question regarding an individual's right to live. Such notions of reciprocity become increasingly evident for women at stage 2. The Golden Rule, that one should treat others as he or she wishes to be treated, is now invoked as the standard of right action, although its precepts are interpreted in a naively egalitarian manner. This is illustrated below in 17-year-old Susan's thinking.

Q. Would it [abortion] be the same as killing another person who was out and walking around?

A. Yes.

Q. Why do you think that's wrong?

A. Because it's alive. OK, just because you gave it that
life, like maybe through a mistake, it shouldn't have
to pay for it. It's got the right to live, just like you
do or I do. What if someone just came up and decided
to shoot me. I mean, I'd have the right to live, I
don't want anyone to come up and shoot me. It's got
the right to live too. To me, abortion is just like
murdering. Because it's alive and you don't have the
right to kill someone else. It's just like having someone come up and kill you. And so I don't think anyone has got that right to do that. They should have
thought beforehand and think, you know, I'm not going
to have an abortion. It's their own mistake. They
don't have to keep it. [Susan, age 17]

For women at this stage, life is evaluated in terms of its value
to the mother, the couple, or less commonly, the fetus. Right conduct becomes the most pragmatic course of action in the situation.
Another young woman, Sherry, age 17, judges that an unwanted child
would be better off aborted than unwanted and potentially mistreated.

Q. Do you feel abortion is OK in general, then, in the
first three months?

A. Yeah, because if, to me, someone doesn't want their
baby, I don't think they should have it, because I
don't think they'll really treat it good if underneath
they don't really want it. You know, because those
are the kinds of kids that end up in orphanages and
stuff.

Q. Well, if you think it becomes a human life at conception, why do you think abortion is alright in the
first three months?

A. Only because I just don't like to see children really
mistreated. I've baby-sat for a lot of people who've
mistreated their kids, and they just had wished that
they'd really avoided them. It's just that the baby
has just as much a chance of being killed after it's
born you know, if it really isn't wanted. [Sherry,
age 17]

Concern with abuse and mistreatment, resulting in an acceptance of abortion, is a persistent theme for reasoners at this stage. This orientation, with its concrete notion of reciprocity, is echoed in the following response.

A. If you think it will be better for them [the unborn], it's your decision; if you think it would be better for them not to live at all, then it's your decision. [Ellen, age 15]

Moral relativism characterizes reasoning regarding the individual right to make abortion decisions. The progressive advance of stage 2 moral reasoning over the previous stage entails an awareness of individuals' differing needs and values. Therefore respondents recognize that there are alternate solutions to an unwanted pregnancy.

Q. Well, who do you need to consider in that decision?

A. The baby. I know I would never hurt a baby. But I know a lot of ladies who have.

Q. Do you think it would be imposing on the woman's rights as a person to take away the right to abortion?

A. Yeah, it would. I don't know. It's really hard for me because I'm not even sure about how I'd really think about the baby in the first three months, you know. I'm sure he thinks and has a mind, and everything like that. I don't like to see people get an abortion at all, but if they're not going to treat it good, then they should. Because, in a way it's killing. I don't know why, I would feel guilty. I could never do it. Well, they're always screaming about there are so many orphanages that are packed, and foster homes, and there are so many kids that live in orphanages all their life, and stuff like that. Well then, if they would just let people have abortions like they are right now, then—I'm kind of contradicting myself—but if they would, you know, let them have abortions, then there wouldn't be so many kids in the orphanages. And it would stop poverty as much. Having an abortion after the first three months, even almost in the first three months, is just as good as killing somebody, or killing a baby—a newborn baby. That's just the same to me. But it's just that I hate to see a baby really unwanted. It makes me want to kidnap them and take

them away from their parents. But I hate to see
children in that kind of state. I hate to see people
get abortions, too, I'm against abortions, too, I'm
against both—so—in the first three months it just
seems better. [Sherry, age 17]

Stage 2 reasoning about abortion is characterized by rudimentary notions of reciprocity. Abortion is regarded concretely as murder, and women are relativistic about the individual's right to commit such acts. For the first time, women consider intentions and motivations in their judgments regarding abortion.

Stage 3 Moral Reasoning

This stage represents a further advance in reasoning, as the value of life is considered within a wider social perspective. The stage 3 value of life is based upon its value to significant others. The orientation at this stage is toward approval, pleasing others, and conforming to stereotypical images of good behavior. Women's reasoning about the value of the unborn child's life is based upon empathy and affection. This perspective entails an inclination to view life in stereotypical terms as good or beautiful. These characteristics are illustrated in the following example:

A. Well, I don't like abortion at all, you know, unless
   it's [the child is] deformed, but, you know, it would
   be easier to do it then because you don't feel it, you
   don't recognize it as a life. I'm talking about from
   like my point of view. I couldn't do it, you know, if
   I could feel it moving around, I could not do it.

Q. Why not?

A. Well, because it's a human life and we can't just go
   around killing human beings. I think it's worth something, not just something to be thrown away, at whoever's say-so. I mean I wouldn't want somebody to
   go sucking me out, and tearing me apart like that.
   It's just not right. But I don't know it's just like—
   when you can feel there is a baby moving around in
   you, then you know how I feel about it. I mean it's
   just beautiful, and I don't understand how anybody
   would want to kill that. [Susan, age 17]

Life is regarded as inherently valuable. Therefore, adoption
is often considered the justifiable alternative to the dilemma of un-

wanted pregnancy since it preserves human life. Stereotypical images of motherhood as a natural female role also prevail to make abortion a less acceptable alternative. Ultimately, however, reasoners at this stage are relativistic about abortion decisions because each situation has to be evaluated on the basis of the motivations of the actor and the future life of the child. When the woman has good or altruistic motivations for seeking abortion, abortion is seen as justified. When the reasons are seen as selfish, it is not. In the example that follows, the 22-year-old respondent first focuses on adoption as a more viable alternative to abortion. When probed, she upholds the individual's right to make abortion decisions.

> Q. Well, what if a child is just unwanted, would abortion be wrong?
>
> A. It should be put up for adoption. There's so many people who want babies, and with all these abortions they can't have them, because there just aren't that many babies around now.
>
> Q. If the child is unwanted is she wrong to just feel like she wants to abort it rather than carry it through pregnancy?
>
> A. Well, if that's how she feels. I cannot see, after carrying a child full-term and having it that it would be unwanted. I imagine those feelings exist for some people. I can't imagine it. After the intimacy that develops through carrying a child, I just can't understand it.
>
> Q. But would it be OK?
>
> A. What, to abort it? If that's what she wants, yeah. I mean I'm in favor of those who are on this earth, you know, it's their choice. I mean, it's not really fair to the child, but that's how I feel. [Jenny, age 22]

The source of this respondent's concern is the mother's feelings for her child. Although she has difficulty imagining a situation where empathetic feelings for a child would be lacking, she considers abortion justified in the absence of those emotions. Similarly, relativism in pregnancy decisions structured at this stage arises from the judgment that only the pregnant woman can evaluate the adequacy of the love and empathy she feels for her partner or unborn child.

> Q. Well, why is abortion justified?

A. Because if that child is going to come into a life
where its own mother hates it, or can't get behind
it 100 percent, then I think she has the right to decide to acknowledge that from the beginning. [Paula,
age 22]

Reasoning at this stage is constructed from the social consensus
of significant others. Images of motherhood as natural and beautiful
prevail to make abortion a less acceptable, although potentially justified, alternative.

Stage 4 Moral Reasoning

The moral perspective, previously based upon concern with
significant others, is now oriented toward the wider social order.
The value of an unborn child's life is differentiated from its value to
specific other people, although its value is still dependent upon serving the group. Characteristically, rejection of abortion as a morally
justified alternative is based upon religious or societal laws prohibiting killing. Those more favorable to abortion appeal to the current
statutes permitting abortion. Respondents at this stage also express
concern with the responsibility involved in creating and sustaining
human life, as is evidenced in the following 21-year-old respondent's
reasoning.

Q. Is it a living person that has to be considered the
same way a living person does?

A. I think of my baby that way. I think of it as a living
person that I'm responsible for. I'm concerned about
how it's doing. I really believe that they're alive,
and the person who they're inside of has an awful lot
of responsibility. I helped make it, and I'm incubating
it, the child—because I could have a lot of power over
it. I could eat terrible food, or I could take acid or
LSD and have the baby come out deformed, and I think
because of the situation, because the child is inside,
completely dependent on the person that the child is
inside of, we discriminate between someone who's
out and walking around. [Patricia, age 21]

Because abortion is legally sanctioned, respondents consider
abortion decision making within the context of individual rights.
Value is placed upon individuals' collective responsibility for their
actions. The stage 4 concern with the wider social order and responsibility is illustrated in the following response:

A. Having a child, you know, I think that's a responsible thing to consider. I think abortion is wrong as a mass form of birth control. I feel like this implies that by saying if you're lax about birth control, just go get an abortion. I think that's wrong. I think it creates a lessening of your morals. I would feel like I was not committing murder in such a case, but I think my responsibility level would be really going down, and that I would be revolving around myself instead of thinking about the responsibilities that I'm doing. [Liz, age 30]

For the following respondent, responsible action in a societal perspective includes a concern with overpopulation. For her, justice and the welfare of the wider social order dictates a moral acceptance of abortion.

Q. Why do you think we [women] have the right to make decisions about abortion?

A. Because it would be our children that we're bringing up, you know, and we want the best for them, and that doesn't mean we can just, you know, run around and abort every fetus that might not have a better chance than some; but, you know, there's a lot of people in this world, and I would hate to see them growing up and shuffled around and living in slums and things like that. I think we can made that decision. [Bonnie, age 23]

Stage 4 moral reasoning about abortion reflects a concern with society, laws, and collective responsibility for the consequences of one's actions. These may lead to either an acceptance or rejection of abortion.

Stage 5 Moral Reasoning

This stage represents a significant advance over previous perspectives. Like moral reasoning at other stages, stage 5 reasoning about abortion is structured by justice. For the first time, respondents view life as a universal human right. Life is respected as a basic right and an autonomous value upon which other rights and privileges are derived. For the following respondent, unilateral respect for life does not permit abortions:

Q. Do you think it's a life of equal value to other living lives?

A. Yes, that's the thing—like lots of people have said, "Well, you could mistake it for a pig's fetus or something," it doesn't have a brain and all, but it's got the potential. It could have grown up and been a president or done something great, so I think it's equal, yeah, it's just it's not as developed. A three-year-old isn't fully developed either when you get down to it, you know, but it still has as much right as another human.

Q. Why should each human have that right [to live]?

A. Well, I just think it's the same reason why everybody has the right to eat. Once you're made, you have a right to the piece of the rock, and I just think that everybody has a right to live and not be killed. I don't go for the death penalty or anything like that either. You know what I mean? You know, I think everybody should be allowed to make it on earth, to get here. I think abortion is wrong because of that, they just kill it. Like in rape, it's still her responsibility because it happened, and just because she was raped, there's no reason to take away a baby's life, the life is so much higher. She doesn't have to keep it; she can give it up for adoption, she can do a lot of things with it. She doesn't have to keep it, but I still think it's her responsibility to have it. Like I said, if you weigh the inconvenience it is to her [the mother] and maybe the trouble it will cause her, against it being a human person's life, I think that that inconvenience is just trivial, you know. Or her career, anything, whatever it is that's at stake is just really trivial compared to the life.

Q. Well, one woman said to me that taking away the right to make decisions about abortion would be like taking away her sense of self. Do you agree with that?

A. I think that is malarkey, I've heard that over and over and over. No woman, once she has another life going on inside her, has any right to get rid of it. It has nothing to do with her right of self and all this, because maybe she's holding the child, the child is inside and not on its own, but either way it is its own life, it isn't her, and she doesn't have the right to take away its life.

Q. Do you think abortion is like killing another living
human being?

A. Yes, it is a living human being, and I think it's like
killing it. It's exactly—I mean that's what it is.
Just like murdering another life. [Sharon, age 17]

For Sharon, life is regarded as a priority and a right of each
individual, including an unborn child. According to her moral precepts, life takes priority over another's needs, short of life itself.
She asserts that the mother's moral obligation is to preserve the unborn child's life; once the child is born, she can give it up for adoption.

Susan exemplifies another principled moral stance. Her differentiation between an individual's intentions in committing an action
and the legal necessity of strict adherence to rules results in a consideration of circumstances where abortion may be morally justified.
She reasons that if the pregnancy was unintentionally created, abortion may be a more preferable and just alternative than the harmful
consequences that might ensue for both mother and child if the pregnancy is allowed to continue. She weighs the harmful or unjust consequences of an unintentional pregnancy against the value of a created
human life.

As the following example illustrates, respondents at this stage
not only make moral judgments but are also concerned with the process of making moral judgments.

A. I think it's a question of mercy. It's a mercy act for
the child, for the human life, sparing it from a fate—
It wasn't expected, but the child was conceived, and
there was no planning for it whatsoever, and there was
no conscious action to have that occur, and the consequence of that—the child—may end up in very dire
straits, because it was completely the result of vio-
lence or whatever, whatever was the conception mistake for the mother. I think it's really a question of
motivations, and that's real tricky.

Q. Do you think it's important that women have the right
to control abortion decisions?

A. Well, yeah, I think it's right in certain circumstances,
but I don't think it's right for others. I think that it's
just possible to reach a certain measure of quality almost, as to the woman's reasons. And if they are
simply ones that release her from a responsibility
she committed herself to, then I don't think that's

right for any human being. I don't think human beings
should be released from the responsibilities of their
actions. That's my ethical stance. Because if a woman
did not intend to get pregnant, and she got pregnant due
to being forced into rape, or because she was let down
by her birth control device, which she had been given
to believe was quite effective, and she was not pre-
pared to have a baby—because of those reasons, her
intent was different from the result, and for that reason she has to act on the fact that the reasons did not
follow her intentions. [Susan, age 21]

Respondents at stage 5 view life as a universal human right and
basis for deriving other rights and privileges. Respondents not only
make moral judgments about abortion but take a metaethical stance
and articulate the basis for making moral judgments.

Thus, moral reasoning about abortion is predicated on the belief that the fetus becomes a fully human life at conception due to its
genetic or spiritual potential. Reasoning about abortion is structured
by an underlying conceptualization of justice. While the value of life,
the salient issue for these respondents, varies according to the developmental level, moral judgments about abortion entail prescriptions
regarding the morally justified course of action.

Personal Reasoning about Abortion

The most prevalent mode of response in this sample was to
consider abortion a personal issue; this mode of reasoning characterized 44 percent of the respondents. Developmental differences in the
organization of personal judgments will not be described, as these
responses were too homogeneous to score with high reliability.

Personal reasoning about abortion is predicated upon the belief
that the unborn does not become an equal human life until some point
close to, at, or after birth. This judgment is based upon the physical
and emotional connection of the child to the mother prior to birth. Respondents who consider abortion a personal issue view the unborn child
as a physical or emotional extension of the mother during the pregnancy. As a result, abortion is considered exclusively an individual
choice, and pregnancy decision making is treated as an issue of control over one's own body, reproductive functions, and life.

Personal judgments are regarded as prescriptive only to the
extent that they are consistent with the individual's maintenance of an
autonomous self. Respondents who treat abortion as a personal issue
view pregnancy decision making as one mode of exercising personal
prerogatives. When the moral perspective is presented to personal
reasoners through countersuggestion, personal reasoners character-

istically reinterpret these concerns within the personal domain and assert the need for control over one's body and individual choice. Abortion is evaluated as outside the realm of societal regulation and moral concern.

Personal reasoning about abortion is structured by considerations of individual autonomy. Abortion decisions, like other personal decisions, are viewed in the context of the choices an individual makes about her body and life. Women who treat abortion as a personal issue employ considerably different criteria to evaluate the adequacy of various reasons for seeking abortions from those employed by moral reasoners. According to personal reasoners, more adequate decisions are those that are less likely to endanger the woman's health or physical or psychological well-being or that reflect a careful consideration of individual priorities and needs. Judgments about abortion are not offered as prescriptions for other's behavior, as this is seen as inconsistent with the categorization of abortion as a personal action. Pregnancy decisions are seen as quintessentially personal prerogatives.

The following examples illustrate one frequently articulated theme of control over one's body. Elizabeth exemplifies personal reasoners' belief that abortion decisions should be outside the realm of conventional regulation, and that societal or religious laws should not pertain to this issue.

Q. Why is control over one's body important?

A. I feel it's important because, as far as I'm concerned, a woman should have complete control over her body, and such things as the state, or the church, or conditions around her, I don't think should be terribly important in her making that decision. I believe she should just have it as an option, if she wants it at any time during her pregnancy.

Q. Why would it be wrong for the state or anyone else to control her body?

A. Because it's her body, she's the one that has to live with it, and she's the one that has to pay the consequences.

Q. Do you think you need to consider the fetus in that decision at all?

A. I don't think so. I don't think that it should be considered until it [the fetus] actually sees the light of day. In other words, at birth. That is when I make my distinction for the fetus actually being alive, because it doesn't know hardly anything except the woman's womb.

Q. So what criteria do you use, then, to define it as a human life?

A. To me, human life begins when the baby comes out of the womb. When it is living on its own, outside of the mother.

Q. So that's the important criteria, that it's living outside the mother?

A. That it's living—yeah, pretty much. [Elizabeth, age 18]

A. Somehow, as long as it's still attached to her, I think she should have control over it—deciding what she does with it, you know, it's still inside.

Q. Why?

A. Well, because it's inside of her, and she's the one who's going to carry it around for nine months, and it's going to be a big strain on her body, and she's the one that's going to have morning sickness, or all-day sickness like I've been having—or, you know, she's the one that after it's born will probably, unfortunately, end up taking care of it for 18 years or whatever, and I think what's important is that it's not just the child's life that you're considering, it's the mother's life, too, and that's what I think is crucial. The mother is first. She's the one who first created it, in a sense, together with the father's sperm or whatever, but still, I think she should and does have a certain amount of, well, a complete autonomy over her body and what she's going to do with it. I mean even if it is alive, and it is certainly alive, still, somehow until the point that it's born—I mean after it's born I wouldn't want to justify her killing it. But somehow—I don't know, I mean I don't know why I make that distinction. Maybe because it's not part of her anymore, it is really separate, but until that point it seems like it's still a part of her, and her deciding what she's going to do with it is a decision about herself as much as it is about the child.

Q. So if you had to weigh those two things—the mother
versus the fetus—do you think you should just consider
the mother?

A. I would just consider the mother, I really would.
[Leah, age 21]

Leah—and in the examples to follow, Kerry, Lori, and Emily
—all maintain that the fetus should be considered a part of the woman's body rather than a separate life. The importance that is placed
upon the woman's autonomous choice stems from the judgment that
the fetus is not yet an independent human life.

A. [The fetus] in essence grown in a woman's body, and
it becomes as much a part of her as any other part of
the body. And until the child has left the woman's
body, it's essentially hers. And we should have control over our bodies and what goes on in them. I think
it's crucial. [Kerry, age 24]

A. The decision is up to her. It's a matter of her body.
And it's like a thumbnail or a tumor. But I see the
issue as being pretty much that it's her control over
her body. [Lori, age 21]

A. I don't think that it becomes a human life until it is
born. I really don't because a fetus could not live outside the uterus until it was born. Of course, OK,
there are some premature births and they do live,
but not without the help of incubators. And unless the
human being is capable of living independently, just
physically living independently, of its mother, I don't
consider it a human being.

Q. Why do you think it's important that women have the
right to make that choice about abortion?

A. Because it's their life, and they're the ones that are
going to be affected by it. And you are dealing with
one person's life and then you are dealing with a
probable life, a possible life. Well, which is more
important, you know. Obviously the person that is
living now is more important because you don't even
know if the other one is going to live. And if it's
going to severely affect her life in some way, she
should have that right. It's her body. She has the

right to do with her body what she will. I don't think
it's killing. I don't think it is, because it isn't a life
yet. It couldn't live outside her body. [Emily, age
16]

Leah, Elizabeth, Kerry, Lori, and Emily all voice the same
concern: women ought to be able to control their own bodies. While
they recognize that abortion involves a potential life, they maintain
that the woman's needs take priority until the child is born. All see
the issue of control over one's body as a preeminent concern. They
vary in their consideration of the fetus. Some, like Lori, liken it to
an unwanted body part; others, like Emily, consider it life in a nascent state. All assert that its equality with human life does not begin until birth. Therefore abortion decisions should be made on the
basis of the woman's, rather than the fetus's, needs.

The following responses exemplify personal reasoners' concerns
with autonomous choice and individual goals and commitments.

A. I think it's OK, you know, whenever you want to do it.
   If they don't want the child, then there's no reason to
   bring it into the world. What is best for her [the
   mother] and her life—the baby, the fetus isn't out in
   life yet, you know, and I feel the mother is more important. She should think about herself first. It's
   because it's her right as a person, to be able to do
   what she thinks is right for herself. [Barbara, age
   19]

A. They are going to be making sacrifices in their own
   life-style or in the next part of their life. Because
   she's got herself to consider as a human being, and
   she has her own goals for herself in life. The potential for almost a 21-year commitment of one's own life
   exists when one is pregnant, and I think one has to
   consider, "Am I willing to commit myself?" [Cecilie,
   age 20]

In the excerpt above, Barbara states clearly the essence of
personal reasoning about abortion: that it's her right as a person to
be able to do what she thinks is right for herself. Despite the super-
ficial resemblance, there is a crucial distinction underlying personal
reasoners' treatment of abortion as an issue of personal choice and
the instrumental relativism that characterizes stage 2 moral judgments. Moral reasoners at stage 2 view the unborn child as a life
and are relativistic about killing. Respondents who treat abortion as

an issue within the personal domain do not consider abortion taking human life and believe that abortion has no harmful or unjust effects on another. Rather, abortion is viewed as a private action entailing personal choice and control over one's body and life.

However, once a child is born, respondents treat that life as an issue indisputably within the moral domain. Personal reasoners differentiate between decision making about abortion and the right to kill a human life. Birth and the separation of the child from the mother's womb mark the transition between the personal issues of abortion and the moral issues of life. Once born, the child is viewed as a separate human life, and decisions about life are structured by justice. The following judgments exemplify the coordination between concerns in the personal and moral domains.

A. Up to the point [birth] there's opportunities to do something about it. I don't think anybody has a right to kill anybody else, once they've been born—you know, you just can't kill people, and once a baby's born, it's a person. [Rebecca, age 23]

Q. How about after the child is born, does the woman have the right to decide then?

A. At that point, I feel it goes into a wider issue of human rights and the fact that murder is wrong, to take another life is wrong. I mean it's really hard—I can't exactly articulate the differences of why I believe that there's differences there, but I mean, I do think it's not a personal decision anymore whether the child will live or not after the child is born from her body. [Sherri, age 22]

A. I think once it's born, I think I would call that murder—that's a strange question. Once it's separated from her body, I don't feel that she has that much control over it, and if she wants it to die, I don't think it should be—she should have that right. Once it's outside of the body, I think that other people can intercept and let it live. [Robin, age 18]

The child's physical separation from the mother is a crucial distinction in defining an equal human life. In the following example, 19-year-old Barbara clarifies that the issue is not one merely of societal regulation and the legal status of abortion but an issue of truly moral concern.

A. I think if she followed the pregnancy all the way to
birth, the child should live, yes. I don't think they
should tell the baby no, because somebody's going
to want it, you can have it adopted or whatever.
There's plenty of people that can't have babies that
want them, I'm sure.

Q. Why would it be wrong to kill at birth?

A. Well, it's manslaughter, or whatever. Not because
it's legally wrong, but to me I just can't see killing
a person. I guess I don't see the baby as that much
of a person inside, but after they're born, they're
really a complete human being, and you just don't kill
a human being. [Barbara, age 19]

Thus, women who treat pregnancy decisions as personal issues
distinguish between moral actions and actions of concern only to the
person. For personal reasoners, abortion is consistent with the
latter concerns.

That personal reasoners consider abortion outside the realm of
societal regulation and moral concern is further illustrated in responses regarding outside intervention in the decision. Laws prohibiting abortion and those providing for the partner's active role in
the decision are both treated as invasions of privacy or infringements
on the self. To the extent that laws protect individual rights and ensure the safety, minimum cost, and availability of abortion, societal
regulation is considered appropriate. Laws designed to restrict the
availability of abortion are regarded as an unwarranted invasion of
personal rights. Comparisons of abortion laws with laws prohibiting
killing or stealing are rejected as invalid. In the examples to follow,
Leah, Barbara, and Ginny discuss the legal aspects of abortion.

A. It's the woman's right to that prerogative, and the
government's feelings about it shouldn't enter into
it. There should be some government interference
along the lines in an opposite way, rather than restricting it, making it more available and making it
free or very cheap.

Q. Why don't you think they should interfere?

A. Because I feel like personally the government interferes with my personal life too much already, and if
I'm going to have an abortion, it's none of the government's business, and that's something that is my
right or any woman's right, that's all. [Leah, age 21]

Q. Why shouldn't the government make laws restricting abortion?

A. Because the government seems like any other person, telling you what to do with your body. I wouldn't accept it from the government—even less—saying what I could do with myself. [Ginny, age 17]

Q. Is it the same kind of issue [as laws about stealing or murder]?

A. No—no I don't think it is. It's such an emotional issue. Like stealing is just so obvious, I mean either you went in and you took something or you didn't. I guess like when you get an abortion, hopefully the mother will put a lot of thought into it and decide what is best for her life at that time and everything. They shouldn't have a law about it. They should just be able to do it.

Q. Why do you think she should be able to go do it?

A. I guess it's because it's her right—kind of like, as a person, to be able to do what she thinks is right for herself. Stealing and murder, that's hurting someone else. Hopefully I'd get it done in the first three months. I don't see that's hurting anyone else, having an abortion. And the other kinds of things that you talked about were hurting people. [Barbara, age 18]

In the examples above, Ginny and Leah clearly delineate the distinction between moral issues and their view of abortion. Moral issues entail considerations of the harm inflicted upon others or of others' welfare. Ginny states that abortion, to her, does not fit these criteria. Both she and Leah assert that governmental intervention is therefore an unwarranted invasion of personal rights.

Some, like Emily, who is quoted below, think that there ought to be legislation concerning abortion. However, the type of legislation she advocates differs dramatically from the moral reasoner's assertion that the prohibition of abortion reflects a concern with killing. Instead, her concerns are those that are consistent with maintaining abortion as a personal issue. She envisions legislation that would ensure the legality, safety, and low cost of abortion.

Q. Well, do you think the government has the right to make laws about abortion?

A. Well, I think it's necessary, otherwise, things are
   going to be misconstrued. You'd have moral struggles all the time, it would just draw things out. If
   there was just one concrete law saying it was legal,
   there would be no more hassles about it. Now there's
   a whole bunch of moral hassle, you know, it's always
   coming up before the Supreme Court. The Supreme
   Court said it was constitutional and now, you know, now
   there's still arguments all the time about it. And if
   they'd just had all of the states as well as the federal
   laws stating that it was legal, there wouldn't be all
   these hassles. You wouldn't have to go—I mean, I
   think abortion should be legal everywhere, and be
   available to women of all financial statuses and all
   ages. Now, I think that's really important. If it isn't,
   what is likely to happen is that the woman wanting an
   abortion would have to go to a doctor who is not a
   legal abortionist, and thereby endanger her life as
   well as the baby's life.

Q. Well, do you think the government needs to protect
   the fetus?

A. No. Because the fetus is not a human life. [Emily,
   age 16]

Similarly, personal reasoners' concern with individuality and
the expression and maintenance of self through decision making lead
to a uniform rejection of the boyfriend's or partner's equal voice in
decision making. At most, his role is treated as advisory. These
women feel that the final decision must rest with the woman because
the pregnancy affects her body and because the decision would have
the greatest potential impact upon her future plans.

A. I think the partner should advise the woman in any
   way that he sees fit. If he doesn't want the baby he
   can have his input, but the final decision is up to the
   woman who is carrying the baby. So the partner
   really has no command over the other person's body.
   [Elizabeth, age 18]

Susan, age 27, expands on Elizabeth's concern with control
over her body. Her consideration of the partner's role in abortion
decisions includes concerns with both control over her body and her
future goals and commitments.

A. I think the woman has the ultimate right, because the woman is the person who has to go through the whole childbirth, and suffer the consequences that women have to suffer in this society, careerwise and —I still don't think that a man should make a woman go through with a pregnancy because it's his child, and take the child.

Q. Why not?

A. Because it's using a woman's body and her mental state, which, you know, can't be recovered. [Susan, age 27]

For respondents treating abortion as a personal issue, the birth of the child marks the transition between the purely personal issue of abortion and the moral issue of life. Because the unborn is considered part of the woman's body rather than as an independent life, abortion is evaluated as a private action of concern only to the individual. Like other personal issues, abortion is conceptualized as an issue of personal choice and autonomy necessary for the maintenance of self and individuality.

Coordinated Reasoning about Abortion

Coordinations between the personal and moral aspects of abortion occur when women believe that the fetus becomes an equal human life during the pregnancy rather than at conception or at birth. This mode of reasoning characterized 24 percent of the sample. As with personal reasoners, the personal and moral domains are coordinated by the respondent's definition of human life. The conceptualization of abortion as a moral or a personal issue depends upon the time period in the pregnancy. Characteristically, these women define an equal human life as one that is fully developed and resembles a human form. This point or span of time becomes pivotal in coordinating the personal and moral concerns of abortion. Until the fetus is considered an equal life, respondents treat abortion as a personal issue. Consistent with personal reasoning, pregnancy decisions are based upon considerations of the woman's needs and the unborn's status as a nascent life; decisions are treated as an individual concern. Respondents distinguish between abortion before and after the fetus is considered a human life. Once they view the fetus as a human life, they treat abortion as a moral issue of life, and there are differences in the organization of judgments within the moral domain. As with those who treat abortion solely as a moral issue, the modal stage of moral reasoning was stage 3, and responses ranged from stage 2 to stage 4: 25 percent of the respondents used moral reasoning at the stage 2 level, 63 percent were at stage 3, and 13 percent were at stage 4.

The following example illustrates the coordination of moral and personal issues in reasoning about abortion.

Q. When do you think, in the course of its development, that the fetus becomes a human life?

A. Three months.

Q. What makes it become a human life at that point?

A. Well, either when the heart starts beating, yeah, I guess when the heart starts beating, because that functions everything else, and I believe that starts around three months. Two and a half or three months.

Q. Does that make a difference in your thinking about when abortion is OK or not?

A. Yeah, because after that I consider it murder, whereas beforehand it's not, you know.

Q. Well, after it becomes a human life, do you think it's the same as killing someone who's already here?

A. Yeah. They [mother and fetus] both have the same rights, because they're both human beings, although the fetus can't talk and say, you know, "don't kill me," whereas the mother has complete control over what has to be done.

Q. Would it be wrong for her, before three months, to have an abortion, for any reason?

A. I myself wouldn't, but—I guess maybe it would be all right, if she felt like this was really what she wanted to do.

Q. Is it more justified before three months than after three months?

A. Yeah. [Beckie, age 15]

Beckie considers abortion a personal issue until the fetus becomes an equal human life; for her, this occurs after three months of pregnancy. At this point she distinguishes between the personal and moral concerns of abortion. Below is an example of the personal issues articulated as one aspect of coordinated thinking. Barbara reasons that before three months in a pregnancy the fetus is an un-developed life.

Q. Why [should abortion be permitted] only for the first three months?

A. Because I think that after the first three months, it's living, and it's actually killing a human being, and I don't think it's right to kill a human being just for that, because they can always give it up for adoption, or something.

Q. When you decide that it's a human being at three months, what things do you think make it human at that point?

A. It's got a heart, it's breathing, it's got a brain, it moves.

Q. Do you think after that point it would be the same as killing?

A. Yeah.

Q. Do you think it would be the same as killing another human being?

A. Yeah. I don't really think it should be done.

Q. In the first three months, why is it OK?

A. Because it's just like an egg inside of you. It's just like a thing of fluid, almost. I guess that's all it is. And it doesn't really have any shape, it doesn't really have a brain or anything. [Barbara, age 15]

The transition from personal to moral issues is also evident in respondents' reasoning regarding decision making. Abortion is seen as a personal choice until the fetus is considered a human life. After this point, legal or moral regulation is considered justified since the act becomes one of societal and moral concern. The coordination between domains entails a transition between thinking about rules and laws as restrictive to the individual to viewing laws as functioning to protect a second human life.

Q. Do you think the government has a right to make laws about abortion?

A. Besides what I just said about the last three months, I don't think so, because I think it's a woman's body and a woman's right to do what she chooses. It's her body and there's no way on earth why somebody should have the right to tell you what to do with your body.

Q. You're saying they should be able to say that [one has to have a baby] after six months?

A. I'm not thinking about the woman as much as I'm thinking about the baby, and of the baby being able to live and stuff. The last three months—I think it goes beyond the woman's body. You're considering a life. [Carrie, age 20]

Some women agree that restrictions are necessary even when they do not regard the fetus as an equal human life. However, they sanction restrictions only when they maintain personal control, safeguard the woman's welfare, or preserve the woman's life. Once they regard the fetus as a life, restrictions are compared with other restrictions on killing.

Q. You're saying it becomes a life around the fourth month?

A. Somewhere around, yeah, the fifth, sixth, and on. I mean that's when it looks like something, you know. But I think that in the first three months, it's a life, but it's not, you know, really completely formed, or anything like that—because to me in the last three months, I've heard of women that have premature babies and then they live. So, if it'll live, if it can survive after that, if there's any possibility of surviving it would be wrong.

Q. What kinds of laws do you think there should be about abortion?

A. Like in the last three months I don't think that it should be allowed.

Q. Up until then do you think it should be allowed for any reason, or—

A. No, not any reason. I personally think that it should be the first three months, and that should be like for any reason; but in the second three months, I think they should only allow it like maybe health reasons and stuff like that, or how it will affect you mentally or something like that.

Q. Do you think that the government has a right to make laws restricting abortion?

A. Well, no, I don't think it should be for restricting, not in the first six months anyway, but I think they should have some say-so. I mean because if you think about it, if you're pregnant you have those first six months to get an abortion, and if you're going to do it, you should be able to do it then, you know, instead of in the last three [months].

Q. Why do you think the government has a right after six months to place restrictions?

A. It would be a living person; it's like killing in the last three months. [Ramona, age 17]

Thus, the personal and moral domains are coordinated by respondents' definitions of human life. This is typically thought to occur midway during the pregnancy when the fetus has developed and resembles the human form. Abortion is considered a successively personal and then moral issue. This mode of reasoning entails a smooth transition between concerns pertaining to each domain.

Uncoordinated Reasoning about Abortion

Uncoordinated reasoning refers to thinking that is marked by vacillation and conflict between issues in the two domains. This mode of thinking characterized 7 percent of the sample. For some, abortion represents a conflict between issues in the personal and moral domains. These respondents believe that human life begins early in the pregnancy, either at conception or in the early stages of fetal development. Therefore, pregnancy decisions are structured by concerns with justice, and abortion is seen as killing another human life. However, this conflicts with the personal issue of the individual's control over her body and her self-determination. That these values are treated as mutually exclusive constitutes the crux of the conflict between domains. Conflict is exemplified in 21-year-old Jane's reasoning, below:

Q. When do you think the fetus becomes a human life?

A. Well, for me I guess the idea of it is like when it's conceived, and in that form of existence or whatever, if it is an existence. But I do, I feel like—it's beginning. There's something that's going to start growing. And that to me is life.

Q. Do you think abortion should be permitted?

A. It's kind of hard to say, because it's like one part of me says yes, and one part of me says no. As a general rule I guess it should be permitted if the woman wants it, even though, deep, deep down inside, I feel like no. I just see it as a life, and when you say, "Well, women have a right to decide" and "It's my body" and this type of thing, and it gives me real negative feelings, and then I start thinking, well, yes, maybe it is your body, and you know, I can see where probably I will have to carry it around for nine months.

Q. So do you place the same value on taking the life of the fetus as you can of a child, or you know, another living person?

A. Yeah, I think so. I mean the person is murdering and saying "I'm taking your life, and you're not going to exist." [Jane, age 21]

Jane considers the unborn fetus a human life very early in the pregnancy and maintains that abortion is killing human life. However, she also maintains that a crucial issue in the abortion dilemma is control over one's body. She is unable to reconcile these divergent concerns, and her reasoning is marked by conflict between personal and moral issues. In a similar way, 17-year-old Dawn vacillates between the personal and moral issues of abortion.

Q. Do you think it's killing?

A. Well, it's killing all the way through, but—um—I'm all mixed up about this. I think it's just killing all the way through. Yeah, it's important to think about the fetus. Very important.

Q. How does that enter in?

A. Well, that's the most important part of the whole thing. That and her life. Because sucking something out that big could really do something [to harm the woman]. [Dawn, age 17]

For these women, issues in the moral and the personal domains are recognized, articulated, and unresolved. For other women, moral and personal issues also remain uncoordinated. Their thinking about abortion is characterized by equivocation and confusion rather than conflict. They are reluctant to make unequivocal judgments about the general permissibility of abortion. Their confusion stems in part from their difficulty in arriving at an adequate definition of an equal human life, as is evident in the following two examples.

A. I haven't really decided where its—where the life comes in, you know, whether it's when the heart starts beating, or when it comes out and breathes the first air, or when it's first conceived. [Diane, age 24]

Q. When in the course of the pregnancy, do you think the fetus becomes a human life?

A. I don't know. I really don't know that. I suppose I would say when it begins—I was going to say when it begins to take on the form of a human being, but then, God, it's always taking on that form, from the moment that it becomes a thing. [Laurie, age 25]

This lack of clarity in defining human life is reflected in reasoning about abortion. Failure to make clear distinctions about life is accompanied by equivocation and a reluctance to make judgments about abortion. These respondents are relativistic about abortion decisions and maintain that the choice should be the individual's. However, this differs from personal reasoners' concern with control over personal actions in that it stems from their difficulty in making judgments. The ensuing two examples illustrate confusion in reasoning about abortion.

A. I have no idea myself [when the fetus becomes a life]. So, I don't know. That sounds interesting to me, and that makes it a lot more justifiable for my belief in abortion. I'm not sure what is right. I understand that everybody has a different viewpoint, so you know, it is kind of difficult. I believe in the right of people's choice. [Susan, age 27]

A. I just don't really know if it's all right at all, and if you're going to say it's all right, I wouldn't know when to draw the line. I don't exactly think it's OK. I think that if women are going to do it, then that's when they should do it.

Q. Is it our right to make decisions about life?

A. I don't think so. I think that if a woman feels that she has the right, then, if she can do it with a clear conscience, then that's her business; but as far as in general, I don't feel that we have the right to decide that.

Q. Why do you think that this is something that people should be able to decide for themselves, when you're saying that for other issues of life, it's not for us to decide?

A. That's a hard one. I don't know. If a woman feels that that is the way she's gotta go, then—I just don't know. [Diane, age 24]

As these examples illustrate, uncoordinated reasoning may be characterized by conflict between personal and moral concerns, or confusion. In the former case, issues in the two domains are recognized and unreconciled. In the latter case, respondents are equivocal and confused in making judgments about abortion.

The following classification task was designed to obtain an independent assessment of respondents' classifications of abortion within domains. Respondents' classifications of a range of actions, including abortion, are examined in terms of responses to the abortion interview.

CLASSIFICATION TASK

The analysis of the abortion interviews indicates that individuals employ consistent criteria in distinguishing between personal and moral events, but that they vary in their interpretation of abortion. The classification task assesses the degree of agreement in women's categorizations of a variety of actions or events, including abortion, as content for the moral, social-conventional, and personal domains. It was expected that individuals would agree in their classifications of all items with the exception of the items related to abortion, and that the classifications of these items would be related to modes of reasoning about abortion. The task was based upon a procedure that had been used successfully in other research investigating the ability of individuals to distinguish between social-cognitive domains (Nucci 1981; Smetana 1980).

Respondents were given cards representing 14 social actions and asked to sort them into categories representing the moral, social-conventional, and personal domains. The contingency of an action's wrongness upon the presence or absence of rules has been found to distinguish moral and conventional events (Nucci 1981; Smetana 1980, 1981; Smetana, Bridgeman, and Turiel in press; Turiel 1978a;

Weston and Turiel 1980), while personal events are characteristically described as the person's own business (Nucci 1981; Smetana 1980). These criteria were employed to distinguish between the three domains. Respondents sorted the cards according to the following categories: "This action is right or wrong whether or not there is a rule or law"; "This action is right or wrong only if there is a rule or law"; and, "Not an issue of right or wrong—there should be no rules or laws about this action." These correspond to the moral, social-conventional, and personal domains, respectively.

The items designated as content for the moral domain were the following: killing, stealing, helping someone, rape, and slavery. Items designated as content for the social-conventional domain were calling a judge "Your Honor" in court, driving on the right-hand side of the road, and eating with your hands. Items designated as content for the personal domain were length of hair, masturbation, and premarital sex. In addition, respondents categorized the following three items related to abortion: having an abortion in the first trimester, having an abortion in the second trimester, and having an abortion in the third trimester.

Overall, respondents agreed in their placement of stimulus items within a domain. As expected, the items were placed in the hypothesized domains with four exceptions, as indicated in Table 4. Both abortion in the third trimester and helping someone who is hurt were placed with nearly equal frequencies in both the moral and personal categories. Calling a judge "Your Honor" in court was placed in both the social-conventional and personal categories. Eating with hands, originally defined as a social-conventional issue, was most frequently categorized as a personal issue.

Respondents' categorizations of items did not differ according to mode of reasoning in the abortion interview with the exception of the three items pertaining to abortion: abortion in the first trimester (chi square = 10.53, df = 4, $p < .05$), abortion in the second trimester (chi square = 22.27, df = 4, $p < .0001$), and abortion in the third trimester (chi square = 30.54, df = 4, $p < .0001$). Respondents who considered abortion a personal issue consistently placed the abortion items in the personal category (see Table 5). Respondents who considered abortion a moral issue or who coordinated the two domains were more likely to place the abortion items in the moral rather than the personal category, and this tendency increased for items indicating the later stages of a pregnancy.

These analyses and the content analysis of the abortion interviews suggest that individuals share common ways of defining moral or personal events and that they agree in their interpretation of many actions and events as content for the domains. However, the meaning ascribed to abortion depends upon whether or not respondents con-

TABLE 4

Sorting Frequencies for Moral, Social-Conventional, Personal, and Abortion Items

	Moral		Social-Conventional		Personal		x^2	p
	Percent	Number	Percent	Number	Percent	Number		
Hypothesized moral items								
Killing	92.9	65	5.7	4	1.4	1	111.80	.001
Rape	95.7	67	2.9	2	1.4	1	122.60	.001
Stealing	81.4	57	12.9	9	5.7	4	73.40	.001
Slavery	95.7	67	2.9	2	1.4	1	122.60	.001
Helping someone who is hurt	51.4	36	5.7	4	41.5	29	24.61	.001
Hypothesized social-conventional items								
Driving on right side	20.0	14	77.1	54	2.9	2	63.54	.001
Calling a judge "Your Honor"	2.9	2	45.7	32	51.4	36	29.60	.001
Eating with hands	1.4	1	2.9	2	94.0	66	120.61	.001
Personal items								
Length of hair	0.0	n.a.	0.0	0	100.0	70	0.00	0
Premarital sex	0.0	n.a.	1.4	1	98.6	69	0.00	0
Masturbation	0.0	n.a.	0.0	0	100.0	70	0.00	0
Abortion items								
Abortion in first trimester	7.1	5	2.9	2	90.0	63	101.34	.001
Abortion in second trimester	21.4	15	5.7	4	72.9	51	51.80	.001
Abortion in third trimester	34.3	24	10.0	7	55.8	39	21.97	.001

n.a. = not applicable

Source: J. Smetana, "Reasoning in the Personal and Moral Domains: Adolescent and Young Adult Women's Reasoning about Abortion." Originally appeared in Journal of Applied Developmental Psychology, vol. 2, no. 4 (December 1981). Norwood, N.J.: Ablex.

TABLE 5

Sorting Frequencies for Abortion Items Based on Women's Different Modes of Reasoning about Abortion

	Moral		Social-Conventional		Personal		Total*		x^2	p
	Percent	Number	Percent	Number	Percent	Number	Percent	Number		
Abortion in the first three months										
Moral	23.5	4	6	1	70.5	12	100	17		
Coordinated	6	1	6	1	88	14	100	16	10.53	.05
Personal	0	0	0	0	100	30	100	30		
Total	8	5	3	2	89	56	100	63		
Abortion in the second three months										
Moral	47	8	6	1	47	8	100	17		
Coordinated	37.5	6	12.5	2	50	8	100	16	22.27	.0001
Personal	0	0	0	0	100	30	100	30		
Total	22	14	5	3	73	46	100	63		
Abortion in the last three months										
Moral	59	10	18	3	23.5	4	100	17		
Coordinated	69	11	12.5	2	19	3	102	16	30.54	.0001
Personal	7	2	3	1	90	27	100	30		
Total	36.5	23	9.5	6	54	34	100	63		

*Percentages may not equal 100 because of rounding.

Note: Uncoordinated reasoners were omitted because of the small number of respondents.

60

sider the fetus a life and their resulting concerns with either issues of life or issues of personal choice. When the fetus is considered a life at conception, abortion is seen as a moral issue of life. When the fetus is seen as a life at birth, abortion is treated as a personal issue of autonomy and self-determination. When the fetus is considered to achieve human status midway through the pregnancy, abortion is seen as both a personal and moral issue; abortion entails coordination between issues in the two domains. Issues in the two domains may also be in conflict and remain unreconciled, or they may be confused.

NOTES

1. The frequency of agency clientele participating in the study and the distribution of subjects' ages compared with the general clinic populations were assessed to obtain an estimate of the volunteer effects in subject selection. These analyses revealed that participation rates were quite low (with one exception, approximately 10 percent of the confirmed pregnancies at each agency), and that participants were significantly younger than the general clinic populations. However, the exclusion of married women and women with repeat pregnancies from the study may provide a partial account of these factors. Unfortunately, data on marital status or parity were not available from any of the agencies.

2. In addition, 20 first-pregnant women having abortions and 9 first-pregnant women continuing their unwanted pregnancies were included in the study to assess the effects of research involvement on decisions and actions. These respondents were not interviewed, but their initial intentions regarding their unwanted pregnancy and subsequent actions or changes in decisions were obtained.

3. Kohlberg et al.'s (1976) standard scoring scheme was employed in scoring hypothetical moral judgment dilemmas.

4. Two protocols could not be scored according to this scheme and were eliminated, resulting in a total of 68 (98 percent) scored protocols.

4

WOMEN'S
DECISION MAKING
ABOUT ABORTION

The reasoning described in the previous chapter was assessed in the naturally occurring context of decision making regarding unwanted pregnancy. This chapter considers the relationship between reasoning in the decision-making context and the choice to continue or terminate the pregnancy.

Relationships between reasoning and actual choices have been traditionally problematic for psychologists, and the explanatory power of structural-developmental theory is no exception in this regard. Critics of this approach have suggested that there has been too great a concern with the structures of thinking and that relationships between reasoning and actual behavior have been neglected.

The approach taken here differs from the more commonly employed attempts to demonstrate relationships between developmental stage and behavior. Research on judgments and actions from the structural-developmental perspective has focused on relationships between moral judgments and moral behaviors. According to this perspective, moral behaviors cannot be evaluated independent of the meaning the individual ascribes to the action. Actions themselves may not be considered moral or immoral, and therefore, the morality of a particular behavior cannot be evaluated by an independent observer. Rather, action choices must be understood in the context of their relationship to the judgment process. Individuals at each level of moral development may affirm or negate the importance of a behavioral event. The goal of previous research on moral judgments and moral behaviors has been to demonstrate an increasing coordination with development between judgment and action, or a correspondence between the maturity of moral judgment and the maturity of action choices (Kohlberg 1969, 1971; Rothman 1980).

Relevant research suggests that while relationships exist, they are far more complex than simple correspondences between moral judgment stage and behavior (see Blasi 1980 for an extensive review). On the one hand, some studies suggest a concordance between the higher moral stages and more "moral" behavior. The body of research on relationships between judgments and actions provides support for correspondence between the two in some content areas but not for others (Blasi 1980). Moral reasoning among delinquents and matched groups of nondelinquents consistently seems to differ; those at the higher moral stages consistently seem to resist pressure to conform their judgments to others' views while expressing autonomous moral judgments. Reasoning at the highest moral stages has been associated with a lower incidence of cheating (Grim, Kohlberg, and White 1968; Schwartz et al. 1969), with the greatest resistance to submission to an experimenter's demands to harm a subject (Kohlberg 1969), and with the increased likelihood that individuals would help another person in distress (McNamee 1977). These actions demonstrate consistency between the meaning of the higher moral stages and the behavior chosen.

Other studies do not reflect this correspondence as directly. For instance, some investigators have reported that the highest participation in the 1964 University of California free-speech-movement demonstrations occurred among both stage 2 and stage 5 subjects (Haan, Smith, and Block 1968). Others report that exposure to reasoning one stage above or below subjects' own moral levels differentially affects behavioral choices for subjects at stages 2, 3, and 4 (Turiel and Rothman 1972). While exposure does not affect the behavioral choices of subjects at stages 2 and 3, exposure to reasoning one stage above the subject's own reasoning leads to changes in behavioral choice for subjects at stage 4. Greater ambiguity has been found in the relationships between moral judgment and behaviors such as honesty, altruism, and behavioral conformity where a "more moral" alternative is more difficult to specify. Not all moral situations contain a clearly more moral alternative, and in such situations, relationships between moral judgment stage and action choices are not as simple and direct.

Discrepancies observed in the relationships between moral judgment and moral behavior can also be accounted for by the claim that moral and nonmoral stimuli have been confused. Kohlberg's stage scheme has been applied to a wide range of issues, including civil rights, marijuana use, cheating, conformity, sexuality, interpersonal relations, juvenile delinquency, and altruism. All of these are not necessarily moral actions. The consideration of an event as a moral issue is not given in the event itself, but is constructed out of interactions. This means that the individual's perspective must be considered in classifying an event or interaction as within the moral domain rather than assuming a priori the appropriateness of a given issue or event for moral judgment analysis. Results of previous studies suggest that not all respondents treat the issues investigated as moral issues. Consistency between developmental stage and action choice may be obtained when individuals view the action within the moral domain. However, this approach may place emphasis on potentially irrelevant criteria when examining decisions considered by the actor to be outside the moral domain.

Most real-life behavioral situations are multifaceted, and the application of moral-development stages to account for differences in behavioral choice may provide only a partial explanation of a behavioral event. Individuals may ascribe moral, as well as social-conventional, personal, and pragmatic interpretations to a single behavioral event, and these different interpretations of the behavioral situation should be distinguished. Accordingly, the perspective of the actor and the meaning he ascribes to the situation must be obtained. The participant's construction of the situation may be a more potent predictor of choice than developmental level in any domain. To the traditional distinctions maintained between judgment and choice must be added the consideration of the individual's interpretation of the situation. The value of obtaining an individual's interpretation of the situation is not only to demonstrate consistency between judgments and choices but to examine the interplay between types of social knowledge and the organization of knowledge within a domain.

The findings presented thus far on abortion indicate that women ascribe different meanings to abortion. Some women consider abortion a moral issue of life. Others consider abortion a personal issue of autonomy and self-determination. These concerns should structure women's decision making regarding their unwanted pregnancies.

QUALITATIVE DESCRIPTIONS OF DECISION MAKING

As is illustrated by the examples in the following sections, women's conceptualizations of abortion are highly related to their decisions to continue or terminate an unwanted pregnancy. Those who consider abortion a moral issue of life are more likely to continue their pregnancies, while those who consider abortion a personal issue are more likely to seek abortion.

Moral Reasoning and Decision Making

Moral reasoners at all stages of moral development consider the fetus a human life from conception on. Therefore, abortion decisions are structured by an underlying conceptualization of justice. The crux of the abortion dilemma is the issue of life, and this concern is more likely to result in the decision to continue an unwanted pregnancy.

Stage 1 moral reasoners focus exclusively upon the consequences of actions rather than the intentions of the actor in performing an act. They are concrete and literal in their interpretation of abortion as murder. Although they regard abortion as a stupid or difficult thing to do, they express no moral injunctions against killing.

Concern with abortion as killing is evident in 13-year-old Kelly's decision regarding her unwanted pregnancy. Her decision to have her baby is based upon a rejection of abortion as an act of murder. When first interviewed, she was in school and living with her parents. Her relationship with the father of her baby had ended. Her future plans were vague, and she had difficulty abstracting about the impact of her choice upon her future, although she expected to remain in her parents' home following the birth of her baby.

Q. Well, how did you decide what to do when you got pregnant?

A. I didn't have to decide.

Q. What do you mean?

A. 'Cause I didn't believe in having an abortion, so the only thing I could do is have the kid. I guess I want what's part of me.

Q. Did other people have any influence on your decision, your parents or anyone?

A. They just told me to make up my own mind. It was already made up.

Q. So how do you feel about having a child?

A. I don't know. I guess I just feel the same. Just that there will be one extra person in my room. [Kelly, age 13]

Kelly cannot elaborate further on the basis for her moral rejection of abortion, although she consistently articulates her adamant opposition to it. Her rejection of abortion is based on the issue of life. As the example above illustrates, while she chooses to preserve the life of her unborn child, the moral value of that life is not differentiated from its physical value; the baby's life is treated as her property. There is also little evidence that she considers her imminent new role of mother.

Stage 2 moral reasoning entails early notions of reciprocity. The Golden Rule, that one should treat others as he or she wishes to be treated, is invoked as the standard for right action, although its precepts are interpreted in a physically pragmatic way. This is evident in decision making at this stage. Life is evaluated in terms of its value to the mother or to the fetus, resulting in either decisions to have a child or to terminate the pregnancy. The following example illustrates the continuity between stage 2 notions of reciprocity and decisions to have a child.

Q. So do you think abortion is wrong?

A. Yeah.

Q. Why?

A. Because it's like, to me it's like killing. I don't care what anyone says, it's living the minute that it's conceived. So I think it's just like murder. I don't think people should get an abortion, I think it's sick. It is. I'd never get one, unless I was gonna die. I don't want to die, you know. OK, just because you gave it that life, like maybe through a mistake, it shouldn't have to pay for it. It's got a right to live, just like you do or I do. What if someone just came up and decided to shoot me. I mean I'd have the right to live, I don't want anyone to come up and shoot me. Why don't you just try to prevent it in the first place instead of going down and just killing someone. To me, abortion is just like murdering. Because it's alive and you don't have the right to kill it. It's just like having someone come up and kill you. And so I don't think anyone has got that right to do that. It's their mistake.

Q. How did you decide what to do when you got pregnant? Was that hard?

A. It was real easy for me to decide. I was shocked at first—'cause I thought it could never happen to me, never! But it did, I thought about it a lot and I was absolutely sure I wasn't going to get an abortion, there was no doubt in my mind that I had that decision. That I could give it up for adoption or I could keep it and I decided to keep it 'cause I think I could do a pretty good job even though I'm so young. I'm only 17. But I still think I could do a good job or else I wouldn't keep it, I'd give it up for adoption. At first, he [the father of the child] wanted me to get an abortion, he thought that would solve everything. But I told him that I wasn't going to do it. And we had a

little bit of trouble for a while, and we weren't getting along very good. So I figured it wouldn't be real
good if we were to get married. So I decided the best
decision would be for me not to even see him. And if
he wants to visit it he can, but I'm not going to be
here when he does. But it's coming now and I'm
really excited. But I know it's gonna be a lot of hard
work, it's not going to be easy. [Susie, age 17]

Not all decisions at this stage are to continue the pregnancy.
As illustrated in the ensuing example, another 18-year-old woman
decides to have an abortion in spite of her view that abortion is killing human life. She perceives the decision as a choice between the
potentially destructive impact the knowledge of her pregnancy would
have on her relationship to her parents and the life of her unborn
child. She chooses to preserve her relationship with her parents.
Her decision making reflects the instrumental relativism that characterizes decisions made at this stage.

Q. When do you think it becomes a human life?

A. Well, it's at the moment of conception, and it really
—it's hard for me now, because I started thinking of
him as being a human now, because I know he's probably almost developed and stuff, and it's really sad
for me to think of it. I guess I'm being really selfish about it. I just don't want anybody to know. It
is [just] the social pressures. If I were by myself
or with my boyfriend, living with him, and if I were
in some different town, and we were OK financially,
I would definitely have it anyway, even if we weren't
married. It would just be really shocking to them
[her parents]. It would be worse if they found I was
getting an abortion, I think. So—I don't know, it just
seems the easy way out, the only way to do it without
anybody knowing, you know, just to get rid of it before it gets big. It's really important for me not to
let anybody know. It [abortion] really upsets me, because it's kind of against my morals, I mean—I
wouldn't do it if I didn't think I really had a good reason to, because it does seem like it's a human life.
Now it's hard for me to believe, first of all, that I
am pregnant. It would just look really bad, I think.
Well, not just that, but it's just not right for right
now. I guess it's just mainly the social pressure,

because it would be a deterrent right now to both of our careers.

Q. So the consideration of not having your parents know, that is most important in your decision?

A. Well, yeah, because it just seems like—it doesn't have any feelings right now. He doesn't know anything. He doesn't know what he wants. I feel like it's a very dumb mistake and it's really too bad that it happened, and it won't happen again. [Mollie, age 18]

Stage 2 decision making about abortion is characterized by rudimentary notions of reciprocity. Abortion is regarded concretely as murder, and women are relativistic about the individual's right to commit such acts. For the first time, women consider intentions and motivations in their judgments regarding abortion.

Actual pregnancy decisions at stage 3 are structured by the love that respondents experience for their partners or toward the unborn child. Decisions to have a child, which were more frequent at this stage than decisions to seek abortion, are based upon evaluations that terminating the unborn child's life would be selfish and bad. Women at this stage tend to view life and motherhood in stereotypical terms as good and beautiful. This typically results in decisions to have a child. For 17-year-old Susan, the stage 3 perspective means having the child even though her boyfriend denies responsibility for the pregnancy.

Q. How did you decide to continue the pregnancy?

A. Oh, wow. Well, I've always been a baby freak. You know, I've always loved kids, and I've always wanted a baby, and I don't really know, it's just motherly instinct in me, I guess. I couldn't really go out and have an abortion. I thought about it, but I knew that if I did I couldn't live with myself.

Q. How would you have felt?

A. I wouldn't have felt like living, I would have just felt like killing myself, or something, because there was no reason for it. It's just the way I feel, you know, something I've always wanted, and that I know I can love another human being. He [the boyfriend] said that it wasn't his kid, and—a bunch of crap, so I haven't really heard from him. Emotionally it hurt me a lot, you know, because I really care about the guy. But as

to whether or not I kept it, it made no difference
at all. [Susan, age 17]

Similarly, the following respondent's decision to have her child
arises from her feelings regarding the instinctual nature of motherhood and the love she feels for her boyfriend.

Q. How did you decide what to do when you got pregnant?
What kinds of things did you consider?

A. OK, well, I just found out. I don't know what to tell
you, I just—uh—I kind of thought I was, but I just
kind of kept putting it out of my head because I didn't
want to face it, and then I found out. I thought—I've
always thought I'd just have it right away, because
I've always thought I've always wanted to have a kid.
We're just way too young, and we have to finish school
and all that, so, I said "OK, you're right"—and then
—my IUD fell out, which was the reason why I'm pregnant, right? When I got pregnant I just figured I'd
have it, and it's just the natural thing for me to think.
I thought, well I could get an abortion and then I
thought "No I can't, I just don't want one." I just
would rather have it, because I love—I just would like
to have it. But it also feels really instinctual, I really
want to have it too, so it—you know, I can't say whether
it's because my mother doesn't agree with abortion or
because it was just the way I feel, but it feels like it's
just the way I feel too a lot. And like I really love my
boyfriend and, you know, he's really happy, I can tell.
He really wants it, too, you know, so I don't know, I
pretty much wanted it right away when I found out, and
I don't think about abortion very much, and I figured
it doesn't matter whether or not we get married or
not, I'll just have it; I can do it. [Diane, age 21]

Decision making among those at stage 4 reflects an orientation
toward the wider social order. The value of the child's life is now
differentiated from its value to significant others. Respondents at
this stage express concern with the responsibility involved in creating and sustaining human life. The following 22-year-old respondent's
feelings of respect and obligation toward the human life she created
results in her decision to carry her pregnancy to term.

Q. How did you go about making your decision . . . to
not have an abortion, to continue?

A. Um—being pregnant came as a surprise. I'm gay.
    I'm opposed to abortion seriously; I mean I think
    that in my head I wouldn't be able to handle it.

Q. Why not?

A. Because it would be taking something away that's al-
    ready going, that I feel responsible for, after it's
    born, and you know, I really value other women's
    feelings about not being able to take responsibility
    for it. You know, I think they're just as valid in
    saying that as I am, saying that I can. [Paula,
    age 22]

As at other stages of moral reasoning, pregnancy decision
making at stage 5 is consistent with judgments about the general
permissibility of abortion. For the first time, life is viewed as a
universal human right and as an autonomous value from which other
rights and privileges are derived. Respect for human life informs
women's pregnancy decisions. In the ensuing example, Nancy discusses her decision to have her child.

Q. So how did you go about deciding to continue the
    pregnancy?

A. Just as I was telling you, I really had to—first I was
    thinking over my past life, my career, what my par-
    ents would think. I was thinking about financial an-
    gles, and I was thinking of the responsibility that will
    have to rest on me. And I was [weighing] the pros
    and cons, you know, how I'll have less free time and
    blah-blah-blah, and then—I just could not make a deci-
    sion on those bases. Like either way I looked at it,
    you know, there are ways to do it and ways not to do it,
    I could exist with or without a child. So I just stopped
    thinking about it. And then it dawned on me, why do
    I ask these questions? I realized it's a gift, you know,
    it's a gift, and it's a beautiful gift.

Q. Did the man have any involvement in the decision or
    did he know about it?

A. He doesn't know. He doesn't know I'm even preg-
    nant. [Nancy, age 31]

Thus, women who consider abortion a moral issue treat the
fetus as a life to be weighed in pregnancy decisions. The value of

life varies according to moral judgment stage and can result in either decision, to have the child or to terminate the pregnancy. Typically, however, women reason that the preservation of life is more important than the woman's needs in the situation. This results in decisions to continue the pregnancy. When interviewed, many women were unsure whether they would keep the child or put it up for adoption.

Personal Reasoning and Decision Making

Women who treat abortion as a personal issue consider the fetus a life at birth, when it is physically separated from the mother. Accordingly, personal reasoning about abortion is structured by concepts of the self and control over personal issues. Abortion decisions, like other personal decisions, are viewed in the context of the choices an individual makes about her body and life.

Respondents' decision making is structured by personal concerns. Decisions reflect the extent to which pregnancy is seen as a potential obstacle to, or means of, achieving personal goals. Decisions to either have the child or seek an abortion may result from the treatment of abortion as a personal issue, although the modal decision among women in this sample was to seek an abortion. For some, abortion represents the most pragmatic solution to their situation. Cecilie, Leah, Pam, and Elizabeth were among the women who decided to seek an abortion; their decision making is illustrated below.

Q. On what basis did you decide to have an abortion?

A. I'm 20 years old, I have barely begun my life. I've spent 20 years of my own time and 20 years of my family's and friends' time just getting a basis for me to move off from, and a child would really wreck everything. It would put a stop to it, and what's important to me right now is the momentum that I've gained from my studies and my friends—and my experience of being 20 years old. And I don't want to stop that momentum. I've got too much in front of me, and too much that I don't know about that's in front of me that will just get shoved aside to have a child. I would have great resentment towards the child, and that would be a lousy situation to bring up anybody. [Cecilie, age 20]

Cecilie is concerned with the impact a baby would have upon her future life. She reasons that her relatively young age and her incomplete schooling necessitate the choice of abortion. Elizabeth, whose reasoning is presented below, also considers the impact of her choice upon her future. She evaluates the effect of having a child upon her and her fiance's careers and lifestyles and chooses to abort the pregnancy.

Q. How did you decide what was the most important reason for you to decide to have an abortion?

A. In the decision figured such things as the risk of pregnancy, the rate of having complications in pregnancy, and my family is notorious for having complications in pregnancy—it's extremely high, and it's much, much higher than abortion. It's much safer to have an abortion in the first three months anyway than it is to be pregnant and to carry it to term. It impinges upon two careers, two life-styles, two lives. A child born now to me and the young man who is to be my husband would be just the slightest bit resented, because of the toll that that child would have taken in my life.

Q. How would your parents feel about you having an abortion?

A. In this instance they would approve because I'm not married, I'm not established in a career, I can't fully provide all the things that I want to provide for myself and the baby, the husband—everything. And mentally, I really couldn't handle it right now, because it would put too much of a strain on all fronts. But physically, except for the fact that it's a lot safer than actual childbirth, I have no complaints. Those basically are my reasons.

Q. Was it a difficult decision for you to make?

A. Not in the least. [Elizabeth, age 18]

The concern with making choices for one's life is a consistent theme in personal reasoner's decision making about unwanted pregnancy. These respondents do not consider abortion taking a human life and do not consider the act as having harmful or unjust effects on another. Therefore, the pregnancy may be seen as an obstacle to achieving their goals.

Q. OK. What was the most important reason for you
to decide to have an abortion?

A. Um—because it's not practical in my life right now. I
do want to have children, but right now I'm still going
to school, and I'm still—I'm being supported by my
parents while I'm in school, and I haven't really set-
tled down, and I haven't decided what direction my
life wants to take or the group of people I want to live
with, or anything like that; I mean, I really didn't
think twice about it when I thought I was pregnant, I
just knew that no matter how much I, in an emotional
way want a baby, that rationally I just can't do it right
now. Maybe, in five years, but not right now. It's
just not practical. [Leah, age 21]

The following 20-year-old respondent states that her choice of
abortion is based on a concern with establishing her identity. She
asserts that having a child would interfere with her goals and preclude
the possibility of becoming an autonomous self.

Q. What kinds of things did you consider in your decision
to have an abortion?

A. I guess my personal identity was the basic thing.
Everything else is pretty much tied to that. Because I really don't know what I want to do, exactly,
and that's part of why I am in school. And, I feel
like, if I were to have a child now, that would definitely limit my life. And right now I'm fighting any
kind of limits like that. It [having the child] would
really change my relationships with everybody I
know, and it would really limit the direction I could
take, you know, in choices. And I don't know enough
of what I want that I would feel satisfied having my
choices limited like that. [Pam, age 20]

Thus, personal reasoners view the fetus as an extension of the
mother during a pregnancy rather than as an independent life, and
abortion is considered a private action of concern only to the individual. The considerations of personal choice and autonomy, both necessary for the maintenance of the self and individuality, structure
personal decisions about abortion. These concerns typically result
in decisions to terminate a pregnancy if it is unwanted, although the
resolution to the pregnancy dilemma depends upon which action is
considered most consistent with the self's goals.

Coordinated Reasoning and Decision Making

Women who consider abortion a coordinated issue define the fetus as a human life midway during the pregnancy when it begins to resemble human form. Until the fetus is considered a human life, pregnancy is treated as a personal issue, and pregnancy decisions are based upon considerations of autonomy and self-determination. Once the fetus is viewed as a human life, abortion is viewed as a moral issue of life.

As most decision making about unwanted pregnancy occurs in the early weeks of a pregnancy, women treating abortion as a coordinated issue typically describe their own decision making as a personal issue. The following response illustrates one coordinated reasoner's decision to have an abortion.

> A. It was really easy to make the decision, just because I didn't want to be pregnant. I don't like to stay home and cook and take care of a child; they make me nervous. My boyfriend is a student, and he doesn't work. We have all these plans about traveling, and different things—going sailing, building a sailboat, and stuff. Maybe in a few years, but not right now, anyway. So, when I did find out that I was pregnant, there was really no decision to be made, you know, it had already been thought out. [Gail, age 26]

Gail had stated earlier in her interview that the fetus does not become an equal human life until it resembles human form. Her decision to terminate her pregnancy is the choice most consistent with her needs and goals. Similarly, 17-year-old Candy considers pregnancy decisions personal issues until midway in a pregnancy. Her decision to continue her pregnancy is based upon her goals and right to autonomous choice.

> Q. How did you decide what to do?

> A. I'm 17 and I'm single, a lot of people give me the feeling, or actually let me know through things they've said that I should have went out and got an abortion, and I don't think it's right for them to say that, or feel that way, because it's my personal feelings and decisions on what I want, and I think if I feel like I'm capable to support this child and old enough to handle it, that I should be able to do it. [Candy, age 17].

Pregnancy decisions for those who consider abortion a coordinated issue are most often constructed as an issue in the personal domain, as decision making in the early stages of a pregnancy is consistent with personal judgments about abortion. For some, pregnancy decisions even in the early stages of a pregnancy are conceptualized as a moral choice. This is based upon the belief that the fetus becomes a human life during the first trimester of a pregnancy when the heart starts to develop or beat. When this is thought to occur prior to when a decision must be made, coordinated reasoners conceptualize their pregnancy decisions as moral choices. The modal decision among women who consider abortion a coordinated issue is to continue the pregnancy. For some, this reflects moral decisions regarding life, while for others, it reflects personal concern with autonomous choices.

Uncoordinated Reasoning and Decision Making

Decision making among women whose reasoning lacks coordination between the personal and moral domains is marked by conflict and confusion. The personal and moral issues of abortion are in conflict for 17-year-old Dawn, and she vacillates between them. Her own pregnancy decision making illustrates her preeminent concern with moral issues; she finally chooses to terminate her pregnancy.

Q. Do you think it's killing?

A. Well, it's killing all the way through, but—um—I'm all mixed up about this. I think it's just killing all the way through. Yeah, it's important to think about the fetus. Very important.

Q. How does that enter in?

A. Well, that's the most important part of the whole thing. That and her life. Because sucking something out that big could really do something [to harm the woman].

Q. What was the most important reason for you to decide to have an abortion?

A. Because I'm just emotionally not ready for it, and it would probably be a heavy trip for me. I don't have a steady foundation, everything's kind of up in the air, and I wouldn't want to go through such a beautiful experience when things aren't grounded.

Q. Was it a very difficult decision for you?

A. I've even cried some nights, because I really feel
bad about killing it. Just killing something like a
baby, that really bothers me, but I try not to let it.
I'm just going to get it over with. It'll never be all
right to me. I don't care if it was just a week [along
in the pregnancy]. It's both our faults. We didn't
want to have a child. [Dawn, age 17]

For others, decision making about unwanted pregnancy is characterized by confusion and contradiction. Diane ultimately decides
to continue her pregnancy. However, as is characteristic of her
more abstract reasoning about abortion, the decision-making process
is marked by hesitation and contradiction. This is illustrated below.

Q. When you got pregnant, how did you go about deciding what to do?

A. Well, it wasn't easy, because at the time, see, I'm
not married, and my old man—I've been living with
him for two years, and let me see—at the time we
were going through a hard time. So [I decided] to
wait for him to really decide what he wanted. These
last couple of weeks have been a real hard time. At
first I thought I could have an abortion. I was thinking, well, this is not the time to be having a baby and
I will just have an abortion. But when it would come
right down to it, going down to the place and having
an abortion, I really don't think I could do it. But I
don't feel like I have the right to take its life. So
I'm just happy that everything's going to work out—
somehow. [Diane, age 24]

Susan's reasoning about the general permissibility of abortion
is characterized by confusion. She expresses great difficulty in
making abstract judgments about abortion and vacillates about the
right and wrong of abortion. In contrast, she has little difficulty in
making a decision about her own pregnancy. She bases her decision
upon personal concerns and decides to have an abortion.

A. It's a decision I think I made long ago, it wasn't
that I made it on the spot. I'm not ready to have
a child, it kind of boils down to that. I think it
would have a negative effect on my relationship to
the man I live with, and on me. [Susan, age 25]

RELATIONSHIPS BETWEEN
REASONING AND CHOICE

The analysis of women's decision making about abortion is based on the assumption that the meaning ascribed to real-life behavioral situations structures women's choices. The results are consistent with this prediction.[1] Chi-square analysis indicates that a woman's conceptualization of abortion is closely associated with her decision regarding the unwanted pregnancy (chi square = 26.66, p < .001). A woman who decided to have her child was more likely to consider abortion a moral issue, while a woman who resolved her pregnancy through abortion was more likely to consider abortion a personal issue. Those whose reasoning about abortion involved a coordination between the two domains were twice as likely to decide to have their child than to decide to have an abortion. The frequency of each form of reasoning found among women aborting or continuing their pregnancies is given in Table 6.

TABLE 6

Modes of Reasoning about Abortion for Pregnant Women Aborting
and Continuing Pregnancies

Reasoning Groups	Abort			Continue		Total	
	Per-cent	Num-ber		Per-cent	Num-ber	Per-cent	Num-ber
Moral	4	1		61	14	32	15
Coordinated	15	4		30	7	24	11
Personal	71	17		4	1	38	18
Uncoordinated	8	2		4	1	6	3
Total*	100	24		99	23	100	47
x^2			26.660				
p			.001				

*Percentages may not equal 100 because of rounding.

Source: J. Smetana, "Reasoning in the Personal and Moral Domains: Adolescent and Young Adult Women's Reasoning about Abortion." Originally appeared in Journal of Applied Developmental Psychology, vol. 2, no. 4 (December 1981). Norwood, N.J.: Ablex.

TABLE 7

Modes of Reasoning about Abortion among Pregnant and Nonpregnant
Women

Reasoning Groups	Pregnant		Nonpregnant		Total*	
	Per-cent	Num-ber	Per-cent	Num-ber	Per-cent	Num-ber
Moral	32	15	10	2	25	17
Coordinated	23	11	24	5	24	16
Personal	38	18	57	12	45	32
Uncoordinated	6	3	10	2	7	5
Total*	99	47	100	21	102	68
x^2			6.77			
p			.15			

*Percentages may not equal 100 due to rounding.

Source: J. Smetana, "Reasoning in the Personal and Moral
Domains: Adolescent and Young Adult Women's Reasoning about
Abortion." Originally appeared in Journal of Applied Developmental
Psychology, vol. 2, no. 4 (December 1981). Norwood, N.J.: Ablex.

While domain of reasoning is closely associated with decisions
to continue or terminate a pregnancy, moral maturity is not. Women
choosing to abort or continue their unwanted pregnancies did not differ significantly in their reasoning about Kohlberg's (Kohlberg et al.
1976) hypothetical moral judgment dilemmas. The mean moral maturity score[2] for women seeking abortion was 319; the mean moral
maturity score for women continuing their pregnancies was 295.
Thus, domain is a more powerful predictor of action choices than developmental maturity within the moral domain.

Reasoning in the decision-making context is also comparable
with never-pregnant women's judgments about abortion. There are
no significant differences in pregnant and nonpregnant women's mode
of reasoning about abortion. Although reasoning and decision making
regarding unplanned pregnancy are highly related, reasoning in the
actual situation of an unwanted pregnancy does not differ from never-
pregnant women's more abstract and reflective judgments about
abortion. As is demonstrated in Table 7, the most prevalent response
to the abortion dilemma among both pregnant and never-pregnant
women is to treat abortion as a personal issue.

Whether pregnant women's reasoning reflects "reason" rather than truly causal attributions (Buss 1978) cannot be answered here, as reasoning was assessed in the decision-making context. However, the differences in conceptualizing abortion found among pregnant women also characterizes never-pregnant women's judgment. This suggests that reasoning in the decision-making context represents more than different coping strategies and defense mechanisms (Haan 1978) regarding an unplanned pregnancy; it demonstrates the existence of more generalizable ways of organizing thinking about the abortion issue.

HYPOTHETICAL AND ACTUAL JUDGMENTS

Also of concern here are the relationships between judgments regarding hypothetical situations and judgments regarding the actual situation of unwanted pregnancy. The predominant method in structural-developmental investigations of moral development has been the use of hypothetical moral judgment dilemmas. These are employed to "test the limits," or to obtain the individual's highest level of reasoning. However, questions have been raised as to whether the level of reasoning obtained in hypothetical or reflective interviews corresponds to the level of reasoning individuals employ when confronting an actual situation, and further, whether people really reason predominantly at only one level across various situations and experiences. Despite these questions from the critics, there have been few studies of moral reasoning in naturally occurring situations of conflict and choice entailing real-life consequences.

At issue is whether the level of reasoning obtained in hypothetical or reflective interviews (that is, reasoning as assessed by hypothetical dilemmas) corresponds to the level of reasoning individuals employ in a real-life situation, and further, whether people really reason predominantly at only one level across various situations and experiences.

At least two contradictory predictions have been made regarding the relationship between hypothetical and real-life meaning. In his early work on moral judgments, Piaget (1932) suggested that all knowledge is first worked out on the plane of action, and that only later can it be articulated as reflective and theoretical knowledge. However, in a later work, Piaget (1976) suggested that an individual's hypothetical knowledge might be expected to be more developmentally advanced than knowledge constructed in real-life situations.

Authors have suggested that treating judgment and action as two separate systems creates an artificial dichotomy (Damon 1977; Furth 1978), and that thought and action should be treated as inseparable aspects, expressed in different contexts, of the individual's social knowledge. According to this view, the type of knowledge elicited in hypothetical dilemmas may be considered more theoretical, reflective knowledge, while the type of knowledge elicited in real-life situations may be seen as practical, active knowledge. The question then becomes whether the knowledge tapped in hypothetical contexts differs from the knowledge tapped in real-life situations (Damon 1977). According to this perspective, parallels between active and reflective reasoning within a domain would be expected.

The limited experimental evidence that bears on the relationship between hypothetical and actual judgments reveals that these relationships are complex. When reasoning about hypothetical as compared with actual dilemmas, patterns of both higher and lower stage use have been found (Damon 1977; Haan 1975, 1978). In general, high consistency between the two types of measures has not been obtained. However, the comparison of moral thought about actual and hypothetical situations may have been confounded by the inclusion of nonmoral stimuli.

The conceptual domain approach to social reasoning suggests that there should be systematic relationships within a domain between reasoning about real-life and hypothetical dilemmas, but that reasoning in one domain would not be predictive of reasoning in another domain. The dilemma of women confronting an unwanted pregnancy provides a naturally occurring context in which to examine these hypotheses regarding relationships between reflective and actual judgments.

According to the present formulation, reasoning about issues in one domain should be characterized by a coherence or unity of organization. This means that reasoning about different problems within the same domain should be related. However, as the domains are not seen as structurally interrelated, reasoning in one domain would not be expected to predict reasoning in another domain. Accordingly, women who consider abortion a personal issue would not be expected to differ from women who consider abortion a moral issue in their reasoning about hypothetical moral judgment dilemmas.

As predicted, pregnant women employing different modes of reasoning about abortion did not differ in their reasoning about hypothetical moral judgment dilemmas. However, with never-pregnant women included in the analysis, women who considered abortion a personal issue were significantly higher in their level of moral reasoning than the other women, as assessed via hypothetical moral judgment dilemmas. The mean moral maturity score for personal reasoners was 348, while the average moral maturity score of moral, coordinated, or uncoordinated reasoners was 293, 304, 323, respectively. While the basis for this finding is unclear, it may reflect differences in educational background among women in this sample rather than differences in moral reasoning between pregnant and never-pregnant women per se. Thus, women who consider abortion a personal issue cannot be considered less adequate moral reasoners when reasoning about issues they consider appropriately within the moral domain. Further, moral maturity does not predict women's judgments about abortion.

It was also expected that moral judgments about abortion would be strongly related to moral judgments about hypothetical issues, but that when moral and nonmoral judgments were confused, the relationship between hypothetical and actual judgments would be attenuated. That is, personal responses to the abortion interview treated as moral judgments should bear no systematic relationship to judgments about hypothetical moral judgment dilemmas.

The results are consistent with this prediction. Moral maturity scores based on Kohlberg's hypothetical dilemmas and moral reasoning about the actual abortion dilemma were highly related ($r = .70$ $p < .001$). Differences between hypothetical and actual judgments were within one adjacent stage, and there was no systematic pattern to the differences.

Nonmoral reasoning about abortion (that is, personal, coordinated, and uncoordinated responses) was scored as though it were moral reasoning and was comparable to moral reasoning about hypothetical dilemmas. As expected, the relationship was significantly ($p < .01$) reduced. Hypothetical moral judgments and actual nonmoral judgments about abortion scored for moral reasoning were not significantly related ($r = .23$, ns).

Thus, as predicted, the distinction between moral and nonmoral judgments results in very powerful associations between hypothetical and actual moral judgments. However, when moral and nonmoral judgments are confused and the moral domain is overgeneralized to nonmoral stimuli, this relationship is obscured.

CORRELATES OF REASONING

Previous research on pregnancy decision making suggests the importance of demographic variables and, in particular, education and religion in relation to women's decisions regarding unwanted pregnancy (Evans, Selstad, and Welcher 1976; Smetana and Adler 1979; Steinhoff, Smith, and Diamond 1972). In the present study, women choosing abortion did not differ from women choosing to continue their pregnancies in religious background, but they did differ in educational background and religious attendance. The findings presented in this chapter also suggest that they differed in reasoning and that reasoning was strongly related to action choices. The path analysis described below compares the relative strength of demographic and reasoning variables in predicting decision making about abortion.

Path analysis (Kerlinger and Pedhazur 1973) employs the method of regression to examine whether data are consistent with an explanatory model.[3] It was expected that while demographic variables, particularly education and religious attendance, would be related to reasoning, they would affect decisions only indirectly through their effect on reasoning—that is, it was expected that the effects of demographic variables would be mediated by reasoning. According to this model, the domain of reasoning would be expected to be the most direct and powerful predictor of women's decisions to continue or terminate a pregnancy.

Age, mother's education, education, religious background (scored as Catholic versus all else), and religious attendance were all found to have a significant effect on reasoning. Together these variables accounted for nearly half (41 percent) of the variance in reasoning about abortion (R = .64). Of these four variables, religious background alone was the strongest predictor of reasoning; it accounted for 21 percent of the variance in reasoning. Those who considered abortion a moral issue were more likely to come from Catholic backgrounds, while those who considered abortion a personal issue were more likely to come from Protestant or Jewish homes.

Nonetheless, decisions were largely predicted by reasoning alone; this variable accounted for 41 percent of the variance in decisions. Education, mother's education, and age all had a significant effect but added little to the overall prediction of decisions. Together, reasoning and demographic variables accounted for over half (54 percent) of the variance (R = .74) in choice. Religious background and religious attendance had no direct effect on decisions; their effect was entirely mediated through reasoning.[4] The results of the analysis are depicted graphically in Figure 1.

The analysis indicates that demographic variables such as educational level, mother's educational level, and religious background, which are traditionally associated with decision making about abortion, are related—although complexly—to reasoning and decision making. Religious background is directly related to women's conceptualizations of abortion but not to decisions. While Catholics are more likely to consider abortion a moral issue, and moral reasoners are more likely to choose to continue a pregnancy, Catholics are not more likely to continue a pregnancy than to seek an abortion. In contrast, more educated women are more likely to consider abortion a personal rather than a moral issue, and they are also more likely than other women to have an abortion.

Demographic variables such as religion, religiosity, and mother's education affect reasoning to the extent that they influence

FIGURE 1

Path Diagram of the Effects of Demographic Variables and
Reasoning on Intention

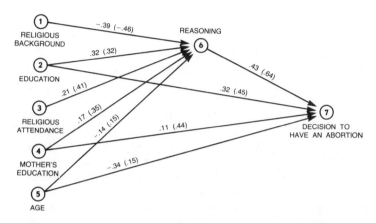

Note: Numbers in parentheses represent first-order correlation coefficients; numbers outside parentheses represent path coefficients. Only significant paths are drawn.

the individual's categorization of abortion. However, as reflected in
the close correspondence between judgments about hypothetical moral
dilemmas and actual moral judgments about abortion, the way individuals organize, or represent, issues within each domain is a product of the individual's development. Thus, reasoning about abortion
does not reflect the direct internalization of parental or religious
values, but rather an interaction between those values and the active,
constructive processes of development.

The conceptual domain analysis described herein also suggests
that the meaning ascribed to an unwanted pregnancy is strongly related to a woman's choice to continue or terminate a pregnancy. Her
mode of reasoning about abortion is a better predictor of whether she
will continue or terminate an unwanted pregnancy than either developmental maturity within the moral domain or the demographic variables
that are traditionally associated with abortion choices. Not only do
the conceptual domain distinctions described here provide a more
comprehensive understanding of women's reasoning about abortion
but they also clarify traditionally problematic relationships between
judgment and behavior and between hypothetical and actual judgments.
The findings presented in this chapter suggest that an individual acts
in accordance with the meaning she ascribes to the situation. When

the abortion situation is defined as a moral issue of life, women are more likely to continue the pregnancy. When it is defined as a situation of personal choice, women are more likely to have an abortion.

NOTES

1. In studies examining relationships between judgments and behaviors, stated intentions are often employed as indexes of behavior without sufficient regard to whether or not respondents actually act on the basis of their intentions. In this study, women were interviewed shortly after confirmation of their pregnancies but before obtaining an abortion. Intention as stated in the interviews was therefore compared with subsequent actions. Women were recontacted several weeks after their interview to determine whether or not they had actually terminated their pregnancy. Behavioral intentions and actions were found to be equivalent for both the interviewed respondents and the 29 pregnant women in the noninterviewed comparison group. All women who stated at the conclusion of the interview that they planned to seek an abortion actually had an abortion. Women who intended to carry their pregnancies to term had not changed their minds one to two months later. (While this does not preclude the possibility of a second-trimester abortion, the likelihood of seeking an abortion was greatly reduced.) Further, the abortion interview had no adverse effects on women's intentions regarding unwanted pregnancy, as judged by the comparison of interviewed and noninterviewed women.

2. These scores represent the percentage of the subject's use of each stage multiplied by that stage's numerical designation summed across the stages and multiplied by 100. This produces a score ranging from 100 to 600 for each subject.

3. Although there are a number of assumptions that underlie the use of path analysis, the present data were considered appropriate for this method of analysis. Its use requires that the predicted causal flow be unidirectional (recursive), that the measured variables be uncorrelated, and that the variables are measured on an interval scale. Boyle (1970) has compared the use of noninterval variables scored as dummy variables with the use of interval scale variables and found them to be comparable. Accordingly, in these analyses, reasoning was scored as a dummy variable.

4. Path coefficients for religious background, education, religious attendance, mother's education, and age were -0.39, 0.32, 0.21, 0.17, and 0.14, respectively.

5

STABILITY, CHANGE, AND DEVELOPMENT IN WOMEN'S REASONING

This chapter describes stability and change in reasoning about abortion assessed in the naturally occurring context of conflict and choice regarding unwanted pregnancy. Through a longitudinal study of reasoning, one aspect of the ongoing interaction of reasoning and decision making was examined. Women were reinterviewed approximately one year after they made their decisions to continue or terminate their unwanted pregnancies to explore the impact of different resolutions to the pregnancy dilemma on thinking about abortion.

Reasoning is examined here for three types of change: change in attitude toward abortion, change in domain of judgment, and change in level of moral reasoning. Only the latter can be considered a developmental change.

According to the conception of development employed here, each stage of development represents a construction that is generated from the individual's attempts to organize social experience. Changes in knowledge are not the result of the internalization of values nor the innate biological capacities of the individual but of active construction. Piaget states this as follows: "Knowledge, at its origin, neither arises from objects nor from the subject, but from interactions . . . between the subject and those objects" (1970b, p. 704). The individual is viewed as actively constructing knowledge in his attempts to understand the social world. While stages describe the form of the individual's interaction with the environment, the interactions themselves are the source of progressive transformations in stage. The conception of the individual as a self-regulating organism entails the notion that individuals' interactions with the environment become progressively more stable or equilibrated. Thus, development is seen as a process of self-regulated "progressive equilibration" (Langer 1969; Piaget 1970b; Turiel 1969, 1972).

There are two interrelated aspects to this principle of equilibration. The first refers to equilibrium within structures. Stages are organized ways of representing the world, and each stage is more internally consistent than the previous one. The second aspect refers to equilibrium in interactions with the environment. With each new stage there is an increased capacity to perceive and interact with problems within that domain and to resolve conflicts that may arise.

Stage change occurs if the existing structure is inadequate to solve new problems or dilemmas. The heightened disequilibrium, manifested as conflict or confusion, leads to compensatory activity that could result in a transformation to a new, more adequate stage of reasoning. Conflict or disequilibrium may originate from several sources. First, conflict may be environmentally stimulated. Not only may social environments differ in the extent to which they stimulate development, but the same social environment may differentially result in conflicts for individuals at different developmental levels. Disequilibrium may also arise within the individual's structures, that is, be internally produced. While stages are defined as unitary wholes, children and adolescents have typically been found to employ a mixture of stages in making moral judgments. Characteristically, they will reason predominantly at one stage and use lesser amounts of reasoning at the adjoining stages. Periods of greater stage mixture are characterized by faster development (Turiel 1969, 1972). Thus, disequilibrium and development may result from the conflicts involved in stage mixture.

Stage change entails the gradual reorganization of existing content of one stage into the structure of the next. Kohlberg and his colleagues (Kramer 1968) have estimated that the normal process of stage change takes approximately three years. Developmental changes in moral judgment are examined here over a one-year period. Therefore, only slight changes in moral reasoning would be expected. However, if, as the findings of the previous chapter suggest, individuals structure different moral issues at the same stage, the development of moral reasoning about standardized hypothetical dilemmas and moral reasoning about abortion should occur at the same rate.

The second type of change to be explored is change in domain of reasoning. The principle of disequilibration may also describe the reorganization of concepts across domains. Conflict may be externally produced through the situational factors that facilitate or constrain the implementation of women's choices. Conflict may also be internally generated through discrepancies that arise between existing patterns of thinking and new information or insight resulting from the experience. Either type of conflict could produce changes in women's conceptualization of abortion. The process of deformation and reformation of structures that characterize the process of stage change

(Turiel 1974) may also characterize changes in domain of reasoning. Although individuals would be expected to employ the same criteria in defining each domain, actual experience with the abortion dilemma might result in different interpretations of abortion.

In the initial interviews, reasoning about the general issues of abortion was consistent with decision making. Although the decision-making process aroused some uncertainty, anxiety, and stress, women's reasoning was not typically characterized by cognitive disorganization or conflict that might be predictive of significant changes in conceptualization of abortion. Interviews were conducted as close as possible to the confirmation of pregnancy to minimize the occurrence of changes in thinking prior to the interview. When reasoning is characterized by consistency and coherence, as was the case for the majority of women interviewed, no significant changes in domain of judgment would be expected over time. Rather, the process of decision making would be expected to solidify reasoning within a domain.

Only a very small proportion of women's reasoning was initially characterized by conflict. While the uncoordinated reasoning category may not provide a sufficiently sensitive index of conflict, it does provide a basis for preliminary hypotheses regarding the likelihood of change. Based upon the conception of developmental change articulated above, uncoordinated reasoning appears to be less equilibrated and more unstable than the other forms of reasoning described. Therefore women whose reasoning was uncoordinated appeared to be more susceptible to change in reasoning than other women. Successful resolution of pregnancy among uncoordinated reasoners should entail changes to more stable modes of thinking.

Change in attitude toward abortion is also examined here. This type of change refers to changes in opinions regarding the general acceptability of abortion and is considered independent of the other changes in reasoning. Reasoning may be structured within the same domain and at the same developmental level, but attitudes toward abortion may change as a result of experience.

The following longitudinal study of women's reasoning about abortion examines transformations in thinking within the moral domain, changes in the types of judgment, and changes in attitudes toward abortion among women who continued or terminated their pregnancies. In addition, changes in general life circumstances are described. Questions may be raised regarding relationships between decisions regarding an unwanted pregnancy and later adjustment. Some authors have observed change manifested as psychological disturbance and maladjustment (Ford, Castelnuovo-Tedesco, and Long 1972; Osofsky and Osofsky 1972; Peck and Marcus 1966; Simon and Senturia 1966; Simon, Senturia, and Rothman 1967; Simon et al. 1969). Others have more recently suggested that the conflict engendered by unwanted pregnancy can lead to growth and development (Belenky 1977; Gilligan and Belenky 1980; Hatcher 1973; Margolis et al. 1971; Monsour and Stewart 1973; Payne et al. 1976; Perez-Reyes and Falk 1969; Schaeffer and Pine 1972; Smith 1973). The decision's effects on self-reports of adjustment are also explored here. To facilitate comparisons, methods developed in the previous study are employed.

RESEARCH PROCEDURES

Women were located and recontacted 12 to 18 months following the initial interviews and asked to participate in a second interview. A number of women could not be located or had moved out of town in the interim. The resulting sample consisted of 41 percent of the original sample (N = 29). Women who participated in the second wave of interviews were nearly evenly distributed among the original three comparison groups; the sample consisted of 44 percent of originally interviewed women who terminated their pregnancies, 39 percent of originally interviewed women who had chosen to continue their pregnancies, and 41 percent of the never-pregnant women. Respondents ranged in age from 14 to 29 and were, on the average, 19.90 years old. This subset of reinterviewed women was representative of the original sample in age, education, religiosity, and religious affiliation.

Follow-up interviews took place primarily at the women's homes. During the approximately two-hour interview, women were asked about abortion and hypothetical moral problems. The semi-structured abortion interview probed women's responses to their decisions, their experiences in the intervening year, and changes in thinking about pregnancy resolution. The moral and personal issues of abortion were explored with the same questions used in the original interviews. (The follow-up abortion interview is contained in Appendix C.) Women also responded to alternate forms of the two original moral judgment dilemmas (also included in Appendix C).

Responses to the follow-up interviews were scored for domain by two raters who used the previously described scoring scheme; interrater agreement in the classification of all protocols was 89 percent. Abortion was considered a personal issue by 41 percent of the women, 31 percent treated abortion as a moral issue, 24 percent coordinated concepts in the personal and moral domains, and only one respondent's reasoning was categorized as uncoordinated.

In addition, women were readministered the classification task described in Chapter 3. This task provided an independent assessment of respondents' classifications of a range of actions, including abortion, as content for the moral, social-conventional, and personal domains. It was readministered to determine whether women's classifications of these events, and in particular the event pertaining to abortion, remained stable over time. In the initial interviews, respondents agreed in their interpretation of a range of events with the exception of the abortion items; classification of these items was related to mode of reasoning about abortion. It was expected that stability or change in reasoning about abortion would also be reflected in responses to this task.

DESCRIPTIONS OF STABILITY AND CHANGE IN REASONING

The ensuing examples illustrate both continuity and change in women's reasonings about abortion. Women's thinking was primarily characterized by stability; change, where evident, was minimal. The examples also illustrate the myriad of ways the abortion decision affected women's lives. Some women reported that the experience had little impact upon their lives while others spoke of startling transformations in outlook and maturity. Most spoke freely of both the positive and negative consequences of their choices and of their struggles to integrate this decision into the fabric of their lives.

Moral Reasoning

The following excerpts are from interviews of women who initially considered abortion a moral issue. The diversity that characterized developmental level of moral judgments in the initial interviews was equally apparent one year later. All of the following women had rejected abortion as an unacceptable solution to their unplanned pregnancies. During their initial interviews all stated that they intended to bear their children but were as yet uncertain as to whether they would raise their children themselves.

When Kelly was first interviewed, she was 13 years old and pregnant. Her stage 1 moral precepts dictated that abortion was "just plain stupid." She opposed abortion because she considered it blatant killing. Accordingly, she decided to have her child. Now, 14, she is living with her parents and her child. She continues to consider abortion a morally unacceptable choice. As the following excerpts illustrate, her decision to have and keep her child made no substantial impact upon either her life or her reasoning.

> Q. You were pregnant at the time so there have been some big changes since then.

A. Yes.

Q. So how do you feel now about having had a baby and being a mother?

A. It's all right except you don't get all your freedom, but most of the time I do because my mother baby-sits. Her Dad [and I—] we're really close now. He comes over all the time and he wants to take me to the movies but I tell him I can't. [Having had a baby] bothered me a little bit at first but now it doesn't bother me any more. She's too cute to be a bother.

Q. Looking back on your decision to have her, do you feel like that's the decision you would make again?

A. Yep.

Q. Why?

A. I don't know, just because. I don't know, I wouldn't have an abortion. That was the only [choice]; I couldn't give it up for adoption, so there was only the other choice.

Q. Why not?

A. Because I don't believe in them. It just seems like that's not right.

Q. How come?

A. I don't know, it just doesn't seem right to do that, they shouldn't have got pregnant. They should take birth control pills if they don't want to have a baby.

Q. Why do you think it's wrong?

A. Because, I don't know, it doesn't seem like you should do that. Not making a little baby come into the world.

Q. Is having an abortion like killing any other living human being?

A. Well, it'd be easier to have an abortion than to kill somebody, but it's like that, yeah. [Kelly, age 14]

Abortion for Kelly is a moral issue of life. As in her previous interview, she is concrete about abortion as an act of murder, and her thinking contains no understanding of intentions or motivations in performing such an act. Her own experience of unwanted pregnancy did not modify her stance that abortion is wrong in all circumstances.

Sherry also initially considered abortion a moral issue of life; her moral reasoning was structured at stage 2. She had vacillated between having an abortion and continuing the pregnancy. Ultimately she decided to have her child, although she considered abortion a morally justified choice. In the following excerpt she describes her feelings about the decision.

Q. How do you feel now about having had the baby?

A. Neat. It is. It's so neat. He's so good. I want another one real bad. I like it a lot.

Q. How has this experience changed your life?

A. I'm not bored anymore; I always have my hands full. I don't have time to sit. I used to have time to go take a walk and get my head together. Now I don't laze around so much.

Q. So has it changed your plans at all?

A. No. When I got pregnant it freaked me out, I didn't know whether to have it or not only because Mike didn't know. I didn't want the baby to be put out nowhere. Without a father. Because I couldn't do that alone you know. I could now, but then I didn't think I could. I like it.

Q. If you had to do it all over again, would you make the same decision?

A. Yes. Especially now. I wouldn't even think twice like I did before. When I first got pregnant I thought about it because I wasn't sure Mike wanted it. But now I wouldn't even think about it, if he did want it or if he didn't want it. It would be hard for me to do it on my own, but I would have to, because I couldn't give him up. If I got pregnant now, I would still do it, even if we broke up I think. I know I would still take it.

Q. Why is that?

A. Because I love babies. I wouldn't feel bad if I had another baby—I wouldn't feel tied down or anything. . . .

Q. Did it change your feelings about abortion at all?

A. No. I think that anybody who gets pregnant and doesn't want their kid better not have it. Because those babies always end up left in the open, or beat up or you know.

I see that a lot. To me it's a life. Right when it's conceived, it's a life. But it doesn't know the difference. I think it's better that it's going to be aborted before it's two months [old] than to let it live and torture it. If the lady doesn't want it, usually it doesn't end up a very happy baby.

Q. Do you consider the first two months of pregnancy like killing?

A. No, because I would rather be dead than tortured.

Q. If a woman really doesn't want it, is it OK for her to go and get an abortion?

A. Yes. If she doesn't want it, plain outright doesn't want it, that baby could end up with no mother, with no love. It could end up being beat up or—I know lots of people beat [their] babies. It's not that they fell out of their cribs or things like that, you always hear those excuses and little bruises and stuff that are in weird places and you know they got beat up and it's better that that baby isn't going to be ruined as a person. A lot of babies have been abused as babies then end up abusing their babies when they're older. I think that if a lady didn't want her baby then she should be allowed not to have it.

Q. When you say that, it's for the child's welfare rather than the mother?

A. Yes. I think so. [Sherry, age 18]

New, more positive themes concerning the increased stability in her life and the love she experiences for her child emerge in Sherry's second interview. Being a mother is emotionally fulfilling to her, and she feels she has made the right decision regarding her initially unplanned and unwanted pregnancy. Her decision has no effect on her stage 2 conceptualization of abortion. Her concern with the mistreatment of babies, which to her makes abortion a morally justifiable alternative, remains the salient issue in her thinking about abortion.

Kelly's and Sherry's reasoning over the one-year interim are both marked by stability in attitude, domain, and level of moral judgment. In contrast, Patricia's experience as a single mother has a significant impact upon her attitude toward abortion. Patricia also continues to treat abortion as a moral issue, and there is no change in the developmental maturity of her judgments. However, she now finds abortion a morally acceptable alternative. In the excerpt below, she details how her experience resulted in changes in her attitude toward abortion.

Q. How did having her change what you wanted to do with your life?

A. Well, before I had her, I really didn't know what I wanted to do with my life. I just knew that I didn't have any big plans. I was real vague always about what I wanted to do. I always wanted to have a child. I didn't expect to have a child so soon, but I had one.

Q. Were there time periods after I talked to you at the beginning, when you either regretted your decision or thought about what it would have been like if you hadn't had her?

A. Yes. Not so much regretted having her, I didn't let myself feel that specifically. I don't know if I was lying to myself or what. When I was nine months pregnant, I didn't feel like I was ready to have her yet. I did think about what my life would be like with her but it did not turn out to be like this, it didn't turn out to be true, it was more of a fantasy, romanticizing, being a mom and having a little kid, going swimming with a little kid, playing with them, and having a little kid hold your hand and walk along beside you, things like that. It turned out to be a whole lot different, it turned out to be a whole lot of work. I didn't realize how much maintenance it is. I mean you have to change their diapers 12 times a day, each diaper change takes about 15 minutes if you do it good. A lot of maintenance that was never in my dreams.

Q. Did it change your feelings about abortion at all?

A. When I first had her, was mostly when I thought about that. I haven't thought about my feeling on abortion recently. When I first had her, she was real sweet and so innocent. I thought how terrible for people to have abortions. I started to think that it was wrong and more people should consider adoption. And then, as she got a little older I changed again and that was when I started to get real tired because she was waking up all night long and crying and I would have to get up and walk for an hour, sometimes two, walk around the

room and she'd just cry. And there were several
times when I felt like I was just going to go crazy
and what I wanted to do, I wanted to stop her from
crying. And several times I just put her in her
crib and held her head down against the mattress and
I wanted her to stop crying, I was so tense inside.
Part of me felt like hitting her and then I would pick
her up again and look at her and she was really innocent, helpless, and had a sweet little face and she
was really crying because she was hungry. I don't
know why, but she wanted to be comforted and held
and she would throw out her arms and want to be held
and I started to think—well, I started to understand
people hitting their children and I felt like I always
loved Emily ever since she was born and I've always
wanted her and how easy it was for me to feel that
emotion. It just came when I was real tired in the
middle of the night, hadn't slept all day, hadn't slept
most of the night and I wonder what it would be like for
people who did not want to have children who didn't
want to have them in the first place and were up all
night with these children that they had and how it
would be for the child. I just felt that it wouldn't be
fair for the child because they really need you and if
you can't be for them, they're not going to have a
really good life when they're babies at least. I think
a lot of things happen when they're babies and have an
impact later in life. I would rather see a child not
born than have a child abused. It just really struck
me. I think I [still] consider it [the fetus] a human
life, from the very beginning, like the first week.
[Patricia, age 22]

Patricia had initially considered having the child a more justified alternative than abortion since it preserves human life. The
reality of being a 22-year-old single parent with sole responsibility
for an infant has resulted in a change in her stance toward abortion.
She now thinks that there are circumstances where abortion is morally
justified. This change in opinion is not accompanied by a change in
the organization of her judgments; her moral reasoning is structured
primarily at stage 4.

Rebecca was, at 28, one of the oldest women in the original
sample and one of the few who treated abortion as a predominantly
principled (stage 5) moral issue. She did not initially consider abortion a viable alternative to unwanted pregnancy and had decided to

bear her child. To her, life is of sacred and inviolable value. Since she believed abortion entails taking a life, she reasoned that it could not be morally justified. Consequently, she chose to continue her pregnancy and raise her child as a single parent. Her resolution to the abortion dilemma has resulted in much more stable stage 5 moral reasoning. Although her modal stage of moral reasoning was initially at stage 5, her responses included a mixture of lower stage reasoning as well; nearly one-third of her responses had been scored at stage 4. When reinterviewed, her reasoning was much more fully consolidated at stage 5. In the following interview excerpt, she discusses her perception of the impact of her experience upon her subsequent thinking about abortion.

A. The growth in me, when I reflect back to when I talked to you, compared to where I am now, I almost feel like, I'm not a different person, but I have matured tremendously throughout this whole process. So it's been so positive in so many ways and of course there are the negative, like the financial aspect, you know, just the realities we all have to deal with. I was really afraid when I first found out I was pregnant. I was afraid of motherhood, just petrified. That's why, I think, my initial thought was, when I went through that trial about the abortion it was just—let's get this out of my way, I don't want to deal with this, when inevitably I would just be postponing growth for me. Sooner or later I would have to grow. If I would have had an abortion and later on gotten married and did it more ideally, maybe it would have been a little bit easier. But who can say one way or another. I can say that I went a difficult route. I knew it was going to be difficult.

Q. Did you feel at any point that you had made the wrong decision?

A. Oh, yeah, I've questioned that definitely and a lot of that was when I was tired, under pressure, I had questions about keeping Paul. It wasn't that question about abortion. I knew, especially after he was born. And I felt him kicking not long after many women have abortions. I knew that my decision was right. Then, after, I felt bad about even considering it, but I did. My question was if keeping Paul was right. Sometimes I think it would have been better with a two-parent family for him, ideally. But I know a little

about that and nothing's ideal. Often adoptive parents get divorces and then those kids are in one-
parent families.

Q. Did the experience change your feelings about
abortion?

A. I'm more against them than I've ever been. I was
always against them before I got pregnant. I think
I told you that. Intellectually, it was a decision I
had made. It was challenged, I was challenged to
make a decision on that and so I went with my beliefs
and I still believe in that more than ever. We're
dealing with a life all the way through. You just
can't terminate that. I know societies throughout
history, some have abortions even way back. I
really felt that, like I was carrying Paul but he was
separate from me. A separate person but relying on
me. That's why I thought this was a separate life and
I would be destroying that. I couldn't do that, I felt,
if anything, he deserved to be able to live. Now if I
couldn't take care of him or want him after he was
born, then I would have to be strong enough to give
him to somebody else. But at least to let him have
his life. It was just something that I feel really
strongly about. Yes, it's a human life. Very human.
It's just in a different stage of development and growth.
I look at abortion like an easy way of solving the problem. Less people on welfare, less problems, less
this and that, but we're not really solving the problem
and getting down to the real root.

Q. What do you think the real issue of abortion is?

A. I feel that they have decided it's kind of an easy way
of solving this problem. I think we have lost the
reverence and deep respect for human life. Often,
we don't even look at it as a life. Often, the reasons
for abortions sometimes gets pretty absurd. I've
read or heard that sometimes women will have abortions because it interferes with their vacations—this
total lack of respect for this life that's within them.
This whole experience of motherhood, I just experience that so heavily. Knowing you're carrying a
child, to be able to say I am going to love this child,
to carry this child in a loving way, I know is hard because I didn't feel much love for this child I was hav-

ing, I was mad. I didn't want this and I was feeling
everything a person who would go for an abortion
would feel. I was really upset. It was very difficult,
but I learned. It's made a better person out of me to
be able to learn this. We can choose about anything
we want in life. So we always have that choice. I see
we do have the right to choose. I can go out and steal,
I can do whatever I want with my life. We all do, we
all have. But I choose not to, and I have a deeper understanding of why that is. [Rebecca, age 29]

As her analogy to stealing suggests, Rebecca considers abortion an individual moral decision. The crucial issue for her is the
inherent value of life, and as she views the fetus as a life, it is a life
that must be preserved. Her conflict during the decision-making
process, which continued after her choice was made, resulted in
changes in the organization of her thinking within the moral domain.
There was, one year later, an increase in principled moral thinking.

Coordinated Reasoning

Randi and Barbara each coordinated personal and moral concepts in their reasoning about abortion. Each initially chose different
solutions to their unwanted pregnancies but, for both, reasoning remained stable over the one-year period. Both felt that the fetus becomes a life midway during a pregnancy. Below, Randi, now 24,
discusses the impact of her abortion upon her thinking and life.

Q. How do you feel now about your having had an abortion?

A. Fine. I made the decision based on what my needs
were at the time and I would probably make the same
decision again. I don't have any negative feelings about
it. It physically affected me a lot. I got really sick
from it. I was looking for a job and I was run down
during the summer and so I just felt really drained and
exhausted by all that and then following that I got
pelvic inflammatory disease and a bladder infection
and a kidney infection that were all complicated by
each other and laid me out for a couple of months.
I had very severe cramps for a while.

Q. So the physical effects were the serious problems?

A. Yes. I don't think it [the abortion] had any effect on
our relationship at all, we ended our relationship but
it had nothing to do with that. We just didn't get along
with each other. My family, I never told my family
about it—I have one friend who I met this summer who
had had uterine cancer and had a hysterectomy and we
were talking about that. She said that she felt very re-
sentful about women having abortions and so I never
told her until about a month ago that I had had an
abortion because I just didn't want to deal with try-
ing to explain why I had done something she couldn't
do and I just didn't feel like getting into it. I would
say that it was a definite growth experience and at
the same time a negative experience. I mean I had
the feelings of being pregnant and not being able to
carry that out, making the choice not to carry that
out felt kind of sad and the pain of going through it
and the emotional stuff attached to the act of doing it
itself. I never felt guilty or wrong or anything like
that, but it was just like realizing that I was making
a conscious choice about something and I couldn't
relate to it as a loss of life kind of thing at all. I
thought about it more selfishly, I thought about it in
terms of myself. It was hard to go through that and
at the same time I would say it was a real growth experience knowing that. I don't see it as taking a life.
Because I don't see it as a viable life yet. [Randi,
age 24]

Randi makes a distinction between before and after the fetus
must be considered a life, although she considers the fetus a life in
a nascent state. Accordingly, she treats her decision to have an abortion as a personal issue that is consistent with her needs and goals.
She considers the abortion a growth-producing experience; she feels
she is taking control of her life and asserting herself by making autonomous personal choices. Consistent with issues in the personal
domain, her discussion of the experience is primarily in terms of its
impact upon her body and upon her relationships to others.

Barbara, who chose to bear her child, makes similar distinctions between abortion at different times in a pregnancy. However,
since she learned of her pregnancy beyond the point at which she felt
abortion was a personal issue, she chose to have her child. Below,
she discusses her experiences in the intervening year.

A. Everybody says that I've matured a lot and I can't
do the things I used to be able to do. I used to ride

my horse. And I can't ride my horse anymore.
Well, she died so I can't ride her anyway. I got
more responsibility now and I can't do what I want
to do. It's hard. But I'm lucky, because my mom
will take care of her [the baby] anytime I want her to.
My mom loves her really. Sometimes she acts like
—I don't know maybe she's just concerned, but sometimes she wants to take care of her more, like it's
her baby, she tells me what to do. I kind of get mad
at it because it's my baby, not hers. It's just about
the same as it was. It doesn't seem like we [she and
her boyfriend] are as close because he said that when
I was carrying her I was really bitchy and now I don't
hardly talk to him at all. I don't ever get mad at him
or anything. He just gets mad more and sometimes
he'll call the baby a brat or something when he's mad
and call her names and stuff. Deep down I don't think
he means it. I think it will work out. We're in a financial bind right now so it will probably work out a
little better than it was. He doesn't like to change her
dirty diapers, but he plays with her a lot. He'll come
home and he'll go right in there and grab her up and
just start playing with her until she starts to cry and
then he gives her back to me. He's pretty involved
with her, I was really surprised. Sometimes she'll
start screaming and he'll get mad and then we'll have
a fight. I used to say sometimes I wish I had never
had her. But I don't anymore because see when she
was born it was like a sudden thing when she was with
me, and I loved her because she was mine. And then
as she lived with me, she grew closer to me, you
know what I mean? I love her a lot now, that if she
ever died or something I think I would go crazy. I
think that was the same feeling I had before but I didn't
really show it like I did. It was hard for me to start
talking to her because I felt funny because she couldn't
talk back, but I kind of figure now that she's grown
with me she's—I love her more than anything, I'd
rather get rid of Gary. Right now if I were pregnant
again, I would hate to do it, but I think I would have
to get an abortion because there's no way we will be
able to afford another baby. We have so many bills.
I wouldn't like it. I would want to know how far along
the baby was; if it was more than two or three months,
I don't think I would have it [an abortion]. But I think

if it was just maybe a month, I would have it. I would want it as close to not being formed as possible.

Q. Why would that be important?

A. Because I think that they're lives to me. It's just like a life. I couldn't do it, I would feel real bad because I'd killed something that was mine and Gary's. Especially the way I am, I'd feel real funny if I did. And if it would only be a month old, it's not really formed, it doesn't really have a heart yet.

Q. When do you think it becomes a life?

A. When it develops a heart.

Q. When do you think that is?

A. As soon as it's about a month and a half or two months. I know my feelings but it's hard for me to explain what I feel. [Barbara, age 16]

Barbara also feels that her choice to have her baby resulted in increased maturity. Her subjectively perceived sense of increased maturity is not reflected in further maturity in her moral judgments about abortion. She initially treated abortion as a coordinated issue, and her moral reasoning was structured at stage 2. There were no changes in the intervening year in the organization of judgments within the moral domain.

Barbara also states that were she to face another unwanted pregnancy, she would resolve it by abortion. She clarifies that a child becomes a life very early in the pregnancy when the heart is developed, and that if she sought an abortion at this point, it would be within (or close to) the realm of a personal issue. Her own experience of continuing a pregnancy adds emotional conviction to her belief that abortion is morally wrong once the fetus becomes a life.

Susan's reasoning is characteristic of the reinterviewed women treating abortion as a coordinated issue, although her experience in the intervening year is atypical. She initially considered abortion a personal choice until the unborn child is more fully developed and resembles a human form. She also considered abortion a less desirable option for herself and had decided, at age 17, to bear and raise her first child. She was one of only two reinterviewed respondents who had experienced a second unwanted pregnancy during the one-year interim; she resolved this second pregnancy by abortion. The following response indicates that although she considers abortion in the early stages of a pregnancy a personal issue, she questions her choice of abortion.

Q. How has motherhood been for you?

A. Fantastic, beautiful. A beautiful experience being a mother. Something you have to feel. Very time-consuming, and a lot of work. But it's really great. I'm still living at home and the man I was with is getting married to somebody else. But that's alright. It's starting to feel a lot better now, than when I first found out. It wasn't working. Why cry over it? Why let it get me down all the time? I'm going to be happy if it kills me.

Q. How do you think your experience changed your life?

A. I guess I just felt that I had someone to care about and making myself work caring about. Does that make sense? I don't think it changed anything because I didn't have any plans before. At all. I was just going from day to day. I thought about what it might have been like if I hadn't had her. But I don't regret it at all.

Q. Do you feel it was the right thing to do?

A. Definitely. It probably would have been the last straw if I had had an abortion. I don't think I could have handled it.

Q. How do you think you would have felt?

A. I don't know. Sort of empty and rotten. I've done it since then. I had a little accident. But it was different. I don't know, it was different.

Q. What happened and how did you go about deciding what to do?

A. Well, I'm sitting here with one kid right now and I'm on welfare and I'm going to school and if I had two kids I would be in trouble in a lot of different ways and I don't think I'm emotionally ready for two of them. Just everything. All the responsibility and everything in general and it would be bad for me, really bad for me.

Q. Did you have a hard time making that decision to have an abortion?

A. No. It was just like when I decided to keep Heather. I just had it.

Q. Was that more difficult after having had a baby and carrying a pregnancy?

A. Yeah, you see after you've had one, you know what it feels like to have this life inside you and it does something that you can't really explain either, it's just feelings. It's really beautiful to carry a baby and then have one and everything, it's fantastic.

Q. How did you feel when you had the abortion?

A. It wasn't like a life to me because I never felt it. It was just something that was there, nothing. Except for up here somewhere.

Q. How far along were you when you had the abortion?

A. About 9 weeks. That was one difference; I was about two and a half months before I ever found out with Heather. And I felt her move and everything.

Q. Do you think abortion at any point is just like taking another human life?

A. I would think after the first couple of months would be where it would really get to me. Before that, I don't know. I guess at about two months it's a life, because at two months they're pretty well developed, they have their minds and their hearts and everything. They are really complete; they're not fully formed, but they're complete, everything is there. They have little buds on their fingers and toes. But before then everybody should be able to do with themselves what they think is best. You go through a lot of emotional things when you get pregnant, and some people can handle it and then there are some who can't, there are some that are really weak and some that are really strong. You have to do what is best for you physically and mentally, and mentally is one of the bigger parts than physically. Because it really affects your mind, it affects everything. You should be able to say what it is going to do to me this way and that way and weigh it out with yourself and see what is better for you. It depends on the situation and what's going on. When you find yourself between a rock and a hard space, it's different. Like I said before, you have to do what you think is best and that's something that only you can decide. [Susan, age 18]

Susan reasons that early in a pregnancy, when the potential life is not fully developed, abortion should be a personal choice. She views abortion as a less desirable although more pragmatic option for herself. Her second pregnancy differs from her first in that her awareness of her pregnancy occurred much earlier in the pregnancy than the first time, thus allowing for the choice of abortion within time limits that were acceptable to her. She also indicates that the pragmatics of the situation influenced her decision. Although her second pregnancy ultimately ended in a different outcome than her first, there are no changes in her abstract conceptualization of abortion; concepts in the two domains remain coordinated in her thinking. Although one consequence of carrying her first pregnancy to term is the increased salience of the life issue, there is no developmental change in her moral judgments regarding life.

Personal Reasoning

During the initial interview, Leah, Gail, and Lana all considered abortion a personal issue. Having a child was inconsistent with their needs and goals, and all sought abortions to resolve their unwanted pregnancies. One year later, they remain steadfast in their conceptualization of abortion as a personal issue. Below, Gail describes the effects of the abortion on her life.

Q. So how do you feel now about having had an abortion?

A. It was very different than I had expected it. It's sort of affected my whole life in the way I just take care of my health in general. The birth control aspect, I am really being good about that and real clear in my communication with other people. So it's harder for me to forget about my body and to forget that it changes my whole cycle. It changes my whole way of feeling and thinking about things, so I'm more sensitive as to what I do, how it immediately affects me. I really like that, having gotten that out of it.

Q. Has it affected you emotionally or the way you think about other things?

A. Oh, I just know that it was a trauma to put my body through, so when I start pushing aside feelings of hesitation, like in lovemaking specifically related to birth control—I'm using the diaphragm and if I start saying, "Well, I'm not going to use the diaphragm" or anything I just cut that shit out right away and if I'm feeling uncomfortable about making love with

somebody I deal with it before I get into bed with
them. I felt a lot of conflicting emotions. Mostly
directed towards the man that I had gotten pregnant
with. But a lot directed towards other people like
my family—I had a lot of contact with my family after the abortion; I didn't tell them I was getting an
abortion until afterwards, but then I have talked with
all of them about it, and I really felt an increased de-
pendency on them and was very lucky to have a lot of
support. I mostly felt my relationship with him [the
man] was gone with the abortion as far as my commitment to any relationship with him. It was a relief for me to get out of that relationship, and I know
that a lot of that was hooked up with the abortion being
associated with the relationship I had with him, that it
was a relief just to get rid of all of that. Then this
respect for my body is real respect for my body and
the amount of time it takes to heal things and realizing that anything I do will change me forever—I will
never be the same as I was before I had the abortion.
I don't think I felt that way about myself before. I
think my whole attitude toward physical changes were
that they were events in life that peaked and then
went back to normal. And now I see them as shaping
me as I go along. [Gail, age 22]

When asked to discuss the impact of her abortion, the most
salient aspects to Gail are its physical and medical effects upon her
body and its ramifications on her relationship to her boyfriend and
parents. One consequence of her abortion experience is her perception of her increased capacity to control her life and make decisions
for herself. She continues to treat abortion as an issue within the
personal domain, as is illustrated below.

Q. Did the experience change your feelings about abortion more generally?

A. No, I don't think so, I think I was pretty much sup-
portive of having the choice about having abortion,
that it is a service I like having available. And I
never thought of it as an easy alternative to birth
control. So I think I'm pretty much the same as I
was.

Q. Do you think it should be permissible all the way
through a pregnancy?

A. I still don't know about that because I've never gone through a pregnancy and wanted an abortion after going through more than one trimester, so I really can't answer that question. I don't have an answer to it. I mean I don't see anybody as having the right to say, "No, you can't." Because it doesn't upset one damn other person in this world besides the woman and the man involved. And the doctor that's called upon to do it.

Q. Is it totally up to the person?

A. Yes, and/or the father; that's still a difficult issue.

Q. What happens if they decide that it doesn't become a life until three years old?

A. Well, I don't know, if it's three years old. I mean, I'm taking it for granted that once somebody gives birth to a child, if it's not alive to them then they will put it up for adoption. It starts meeting it's own needs right away, I mean that's obvious you know. Just from an objective point of view. The kid is on its own as far as getting air and making its own blood and all that. So I don't see the mother having the total say over a child once it's born. [Gail, age 22]

Gail reaffirms that the transition between the personal concerns of abortion and the moral issues of life occurs at birth. Her decision produced no significant changes in her conceptualization of abortion; her conviction that abortion is a personal issue has solidified and strengthened.

Leah's response is also typical of women who regarded abortion as a personal issue and sought an abortion to resolve their unwanted pregnancies. Like Gail, she expresses no regrets about her decision and views it as the most appropriate choice for her. However, she also acknowledges the negative aspects of her decision, both in terms of her daydreams about the potential child and her unpleasant memories of the medical procedure.

Q. So how do you feel now [about having an abortion]?

A. I feel like I'm just lucky that I could have it and that it's all over; you know it's all over now as if I'd never gotten pregnant; I still remember the whole experience but I don't think about it much. The child would be a couple of months old now and I don't have that and I feel lucky. It still was a terrible experience [physically]. In a roundabout kind of way I think it's made me feel a little more like it's another experience or it's another thing that somehow I got myself into but also managed to get myself out of and took care of myself. It was my own fault I got pregnant in the first place but at least it turned out all right. In a way I feel a little bit better about myself for having been able to get through all that, even though I wish I'd never had to have done it in the first place. I just don't really think about it that much. I don't know why; it's not that it wasn't important to me, maybe a part of me has blocked it out to a certain extent but it's not something that crosses my thoughts very often; it's kind of unusual for something as seemingly as important as that. The biggest thing was just the horror of it; I'd be so scared [if I had another abortion] that I'd have to go to sleep again, go to that terrible hospital and have those sterile, terrible nurses and doctors looking down on me, just like I was in a production line with all those other women; that would be scary for me to have to go through that again, but I still feel real strong about my life coming first in a sense and I'm not going to have kids until I'm ready, I'm just not and I feel like I have the right to make that choice.

Q. How would you describe the experience?

A. Probably as a growth experience.

Q. In what way?

A. Well, God, you know, just being pregnant and going through that whole experience. I'm sure there are things I learned about myself and about my feelings that I might not know about now but whenever you look at something like that it's a growing experience for you.

Q. Did it change your feelings about abortion more generally?

A. Yeah, I think the one thing that's real poignant to me now is the whole thing about cutting off aid for abortions, because I'm on Medi-Cal. I'm just barely scraping by. And I realized, "My God, they're talking about me." If I get pregnant again, God forbid, that would be the only way I could afford it; I'm

one of these poor women they're talking about, I'm
just identified real strongly with that. Beforehand
I would have been in support of that, now it's a more
personal thing. My God, I would not have access to
abortion privileges. Well, because I still feel like
until a child leaves the mother's—until a child's born
it's just still her body and doesn't have the right to
itself above and beyond what the mother wants to do
with it. It's still in the mother's body, but it's the
life in it, it's 20 years or whatever. I just think
that's the choice one should have. I still put the
mother's rights first. I just do, I just feel like I
have to, even though I have little twinges in me that
say, "Well, you know, what about the baby, what about
the baby?" But, so what about the mother, I just feel
like that's more important.

Q. Why do you think it's more important that women
make that choice till birth?

A. Well, obviously after birth I guess there isn't too
much argument whether it's a person or not. It
just seems like exercising control until that point.
I don't know, it just seems important. [Leah, age 22]

Leah's thinking remains structured by personal concerns. She
maintains that the transition between the personal and moral issues
of abortion occur only when the child is independent of the mother.
When asked to discuss the effects of her experience on her thinking,
her remarks address the highly politicized issue of government fund-
ing for abortion. Her concern with current legal inequalities regarding access to abortion reveals the sometimes fragile distinction between the personal and moral issues of abortion. While she considers
abortion a personal issue, infringement upon personal choice becomes
for her a moral issue structured by justice.

Robin's response to her abortion is very similar to Leah's.
She views her decision in a very positive light, and the most significant aspect of the experience centers on her feelings about the end of
her relationship with her boyfriend. Like Leah, she acknowledges
some negative emotions when she thinks about her relationship with
her boyfriend and the fetus she aborted.

Q. OK, so how do you feel now about the whole experience
of having an abortion?

A. There's a lot of different things to do in my personal
life that sort of have made it a little harder than I ex-

pected, because I'm not seeing the person that I got pregnant with anymore and we saw each other for a very long time after and before it, and I think the abortion made the emotional ties a lot closer than they would have been had I not had an abortion or had I not gotten pregnant. It was really very, very hard to not see him anymore. And I just seemed to put a lot on our relationship. It meant a lot to me because I had the abortion; it started meaning more to me. I mean I think of the abortion a lot when I think of him. So I mean that's definitely what's affected me the most. Yeah, [the abortion] just made me feel very self-sufficient and just very good about myself. I was going around telling people that I had just had an abortion an hour ago and I was really happy.

Q. Have you thought about it much since?

A. Yeah, I think about it every once in a while. Usually when I see a child that might be the same age as the one I would have had. Uh, it sort of makes me feel a bit curious, 'cause I start thinking about what my child would have looked like if I had had it. It makes me feel a little bad sometimes, but I mean I'll have plenty of other chances so, I don't dwell on it that much, just in passing. I feel sort of nostalgic about Paul, the relationship I was having with Paul and how the abortion connected us.

Q. What was the major reason that you had that abortion?

A. I didn't want a child at 18; it was just not the right time to have a child. I didn't feel myself mature or responsible enough. I was in college and I didn't have enough money to support it; those are basically the reasons. I've always thought that abortion should be completely an available thing for anybody who wants it and it's pretty much where I stand right now. For me, the fetus is a fetus and it can't exist on its own; it's not an individual until the mother gives birth. But on the other hand it is dangerous after four and a half or five months, I've heard, and I think it would really be harmful to the mother. It's her decision ultimately. I don't think there should be any laws; I think it should be up to the mother, but I think she should be given enough information to know what she's

getting into and to make her own decision being well
informed. And I definitely feel that you're not killing;
if you're going to have an abortion at whatever, six
weeks, then what's wrong with having it? It just
seems to me that it's not an individual until it can
breathe on its own. It's sort of in between life and
death, sort of. It's growing, it's alive, but it's not
living on its own. Everybody should be able to decide
things about their bodies and since a lot of the time
contraception doesn't always work, as it happened
with me, and you don't want something to happen to
your body that's happening. I think you should be able
to stop it if you're not responsible enough to have a
child; I think you should be able to stop it because it
can ruin a large part of your life. I've just heard
about so many people going through with having a
child and having to get married. I mean why are
women able to use contraceptives to stop things or
change things in their body? I think abortion should
be just as much available, it's essentially a form of
contraception anyway. It should be available to
everybody. [Robin, age 19]

Robin reiterates the personal concerns that lead to her decision
to seek an abortion and also her belief that the fetus should not be
treated as a life until birth, when it is independent of the mother and
breathing on its own. She expresses reservations about the permissibility of abortion in the later stages of a pregnancy, but her concern is with the medical risks to the woman rather than the issue of
life. She is nostalgic about the relationship with the man involved; to
a lesser degree, her thinking about the experience focuses upon the
potential child. Her thinking also did not change over the year; she
still considers the choice of abortion an issue within the personal domain.

For Lana, having an abortion marked some significant changes
in her life. Below, she describes the impact of the experience upon
her relationship with the father of her unborn child and upon her personal goals.

Q. How do you feel now that you have had an abortion?

A. Well, it's not really a part of my life, particularly.
It seems to have marked a turning point in my life.
I think I made a lot of decisions to start working more
towards my goal where before I was just playing around.

Of course, if I was in a situation to get married, I
would have the baby and since that time I have really
decided that I really want children. More than I think I
had at that time, I went through a big thing of really
wanting kids. It seems like it happened at that point
when things were changing. Whenever I think about
my life changing, I always think back to that point.
I broke up with the guy I was going with and I never
saw him again after that too much. I didn't have any
anger towards him or anything, it's just that he wasn't
the person I wanted to be with. I don't know if it was
depression or anything, I went through a period of
really staying home a lot and not wanting to go out
with too many men. Now, I know what it's like to go
through an abortion, but it seems like now I've changed
a lot since that time. I feel a lot more responsible
and I feel a lot more, have a different attitude toward
motherhood and children and that's one reason why I
certainly wouldn't want to get pregnant again because
I think I would have a harder decision about getting
an abortion although I probably wouldn't want to have
a child because it would, right now, it would interfere
with what I want to do. All I know is that I have thought
much more about having kids and that I really want to
have kids. But I really don't think I thought about the
abortion or thinking I've lost anything. I don't think I
made a mistake. [Lana, age 28]

Lana views her abortion as a significant experience in her life
because it marked some important changes in her goals and relationships with significant others. For Lana, now 28, renewed awareness
of her goals includes a desire to have children and a rethinking of
the meaning of motherhood to her. During her first interview, Lana
considered abortion an issue solely in the personal domain. However, one year later she reconceptualizes abortion as an issue coordinated between the personal and moral domains. This is illustrated below.

Q. If you had to describe it as a growth experience or
   a negative experience, how would you describe it?

A. I guess it has been a growth experience because it's
   made me think about it and maybe think about what
   life is. I mean that's where it's coming back a little
   more, if I hadn't had that experience I would have con-

tinued to be a little uncommitted about it. Even though I think I have definite ideas, I don't know—if it got in the way of doing what I want to do I still might have an abortion, but I have a feeling about it as life.

Q. When do you consider it a human life that has to be weighed in the decision?

A. I guess around six weeks or so.

Q. Why?

A. Well, you know, it's pretty much formed and it starts reacting to things. They've shown pictures of it grasping, it starts to grasp the cord and it reacts to different stimuli, so I guess I would think of it as life about that time.

Q. When do you think abortion should be permissible?

A. I guess up to about the second month or so.

Q. Why do you think it's OK up until then?

A. Well, I guess I still think of it as not being alive.

Q. How about after that time?

A. I don't know, I guess I feel like it's a life, but you know it's like if someone wanted to do that I would never say that they couldn't. I wouldn't go out and fight abortion. I guess because of the issue of life and people taking the responsibiliy. I guess the thing is I'm beginning to feel that we've been taught for too long that children are such a burden to us and the men believe that the women believe that and when you have that feeling then nobody wants to have kids. They don't want to have the responsibility, but if we started really seeing it as a privilege and as something really beautiful then we could have those children and we also might be a little bit more responsible for the children if we have them or for being a little more careful about not having them. It's like that's really not our prerogative to take someone else's—if someone else lives or dies. We're not really the master of that.

Q. Who should be able to have those kinds of rights?

A. Well, I guess I don't think anyone should. I mean that's in God's hands. As far as anyone else taking away another life. I think probably it really is an issue of killing.

Q. How about laws, do you think there should be laws
prohibiting abortion?

A. Maybe after a certain point, there should be. I
don't know, I think that a person has to deal with that
on their own with their own conscience. If they didn't
have to go through the decision themselves, then it's
like we're saying the law says either we're not going
to think about it because either we're going to say it's
right because of the law or we're going to say it's wrong
because of the law. It's taking away the growth that
we go through making those decisions. [Lana, age 28]

For Lana, the abortion decision remains an individual choice
although she now constructs the decision within the moral rather than
the personal domain with the exception of the very early stages of a
pregnancy. For this respondent, the conflict of decision making
leads to the reconstruction of abortion from an issue solely within the
personal domain to an issue coordinated between the two domains.
She attributes her change in beliefs regarding the start of human life
to changes in her goals and awareness. New beliefs about when human life begins result in her recategorization of abortion from a personal issue to a coordinated issue. Thus, her criteria for defining
the moral and personal domains and her thinking regarding the transition between personal and moral concerns remains the same, but her
beliefs about when this transition occurs change. This results in her
altered conceptualization of abortion.

Thus, the most striking aspect of decision making, choice, and
experience for women who consider abortion a moral, personal, or
coordinated issue is its impact upon relationships with significant
others and upon general life circumstances. Most report a subjectively perceived sense of increased maturity as a result of their decision, whether that decision was to abort or continue the pregnancy.
Reasoning was typically characterized by consistency in domain, developmental level, and attitudes.

Uncoordinated Reasoning

This chapter began with the assertion that reconceptualizations
of abortion might be more likely among women whose reasoning was
initially uncoordinated, as this reasoning appears to be less equilibrated and more vulnerable to change than the other forms of reasoning described. Respondents whose reasoning was uncoordinated
initially comprised a very small proportion of the sample. When re-

contacted, these women characteristically refused to participate in the second wave of interviews, and refusals came exclusively from women in this group. They indicated that the conflict produced by the pregnancy experience remained as yet unresolved.

The respondents who did consent to be reinterviewed recategorized abortion as a personal issue. As expected, their reasoning had achieved a more stable equilibrium. However, the response rate was too low to test hypotheses regarding the role of conflict in the reorganization of responses across domains.

ANALYSES OF STABILITY AND CHANGE IN REASONING

Overall, there were no significant changes over time as assessed using McNemar's tests (Siegel 1956) in attitude toward abortion or domain of reasoning. Overall, and according to pregnancy decisions, women's conceptualizations of abortion remained consistent over the one-year interval. While many respondents indicated that another unwanted pregnancy would result in a different decision, (and two women did make the alternate choice when faced with a second unwanted pregnancy in the interim), there were few changes in domain of reasoning.

There was a net positive change of one-third of a stage over time in responses to both hypothetical moral judgment dilemmas and moral judgments about abortion. This marginally significant trend (p < .10) is consistent with predictions based upon the findings from other longitudinal studies of moral development, which report that the average rate of developmental stage change is three years (Kramer 1968). The same trend toward developmental progress in moral judgments was observed in responses to both the hypothetical and actual moral dilemmas, suggesting the continuity between moral reasoning about abortion and reasoning about other moral issues. Moral reasoning about abortion was again highly related (r = .67, p < .05) to reasoning about the standardized hypothetical moral judgment dilemmas.

Responses to the classification task were nearly identical to responses obtained a year before. These comparisons are indicated in Table 8. Analyses performed on the original data revealed that mode of reasoning about abortion differentiated women's sorting of the three items pertaining to abortion. Personal reasoners were more likely to categorize abortion in the personal category, while, as the gestation time indicated by the abortion items increased, moral reasoners were more likely to place the items in the moral category.

A change in this pattern occurred in analyses of task responses one year later. Mode of reasoning had a significant effect in women's sorting of items pertaining to the early stages of a pregnancy but not in their sorting of the item pertaining to abortion in the last three

TABLE 8

Comparison of Responses to Classification Task at Time 1 and Time 2
(in percent)

	Moral		Social-Conventional		Personal	
	Time 1	Time 2	Time 1	Time 2	Time 1	Time 2
Hypothetical moral items						
Killing	93	100	6	0	1	0
Rape	96	100	3	0	1	0
Stealing	81	81	13	11.5	6	8
Slavery	96	100	3	0	6	0
Helping someone who is hurt	51	77	6	0	41.5	23
Hypothesized social-conventional items						
Driving on the right side of the road	20	23	77	77	3	0
Calling a judge "Your Honor" in court	3	0	46	42	51	57
Eating with hands	1	0	3	12	94	88
Hypothesized personal items						
Length of hair	0	4	0	4	100	92
Premarital sex	0	0	1	0	99	0
Masturbation	0	0	0	0	100	100
Abortion items						
Abortion in first trimester	7	27	3	0	90	73
Abortion in second trimester	21	27	6	4	73	69
Abortion in third trimester	34	50	10	8	56	42

TABLE 9

Classification of the Abortion Items Based on Mode of Reasoning
about Abortion

	Moral (in percent)	Social- Conventional (in percent)	Personal (in percent)	x^2	p
Abortion in the first three months					
Moral	86	0	14		
Coordinated	0	0	100	16.20	.0001
Personal	8	0	92		
Abortion in the second three months					
Moral	71	14	14		
Coordinated	17	0	83	13.38	.01
Personal	8	0	92		
Abortion in the last three months					
Moral	71	14	14		
Coordinated	50	17	33	6.17	n.s.
Personal	33	0	67		

n.s. = not significant

months (abortion in the first trimester: chi square = 16.20, p <
.0001); abortion in the second trimester: chi square = 13.38, p <
.01). Abortion was now more consistently categorized as a moral
issue by moral reasoners and as a personal issue by personal reasoners. These analyses are presented in Table 9.

McNemar's tests (Siegel 1956) indicated that there were no
statistically significant changes over the one-year interval in the
categorization of items in domains. Women's categorization of all
items as content for the moral, social-conventional, and personal domains remained consistent over the one-year period.

Thus, reasoning about abortion remained stable over one year
after women chose to terminate or continue their unwanted pregnancies; there were no significant changes in never- or first-pregnant

women's conceptualization of abortion. Decisions to either continue or terminate a first, unwanted pregnancy resulted in more stable judgments of abortion as a moral issue of life, as an issue of personal choice, or as an issue coordinated between the two domains.

Moral reasoning about abortion progressed one-third of a stage, which was consistent with predictions based on other longitudinal studies of moral development. This developmental progress in moral reasoning about abortion was paralleled by similar changes in hypothetical moral judgments, and the two remained highly related.

Most striking were women's reports of the qualitative changes in life circumstances and relationships with significant others. The resolution of the pregnancy dilemma, either through abortion or by continuing an unwanted pregnancy, resulted in women's self-reports of subjectively perceived positive psychological changes. Some reported that they discovered inner resources they had not known they possessed; others reported that having worked through the crisis lead to increased feelings of strength, maturity, and independence. Women consistently reported satisfaction with their choices, whether to continue or terminate their initially unplanned and unwanted pregnancies.

6

ADOLESCENT
REASONING
ABOUT ABORTION

Unwanted pregnancy, abortion, and childbearing have become common experiences of adolescence. Nearly one million pregnancies are reported annually among young women under the age of 20. Four out of every ten pregnancies annually are to women in their teens, and two out of every ten children born are to teenage mothers. One out of every ten abortions performed is to a teenager. Yet relatively little is known about adolescent thinking about these issues.

The study reported in this chapter describes adolescents' thinking about sexuality, abortion, and childbearing. In contrast to other approaches, which place emphasis upon the extent, or accuracy, of adolescents' knowledge of these issues, the purpose of this study was to examine the logic of adolescent thinking through analyses of the type and organization of judgments.

Abortion was presented as a hypothetical issue to adolescents between the ages of 12 and 18 to examine age and sex differences in their conceptualizations of abortion. It was expected that among adolescents familiar with the abortion issue, there would be no age differences in the type of judgment employed. However, age-related differences were expected in the organization of personal and moral concepts of abortion. These were expected to parallel developmental differences in reasoning about hypothetical moral and personal dilemmas.

The discussion below is based on two-hour interviews with 46 primarily lower- to upper-middle class, Caucasian, junior high and high-school students. None of the respondents were pregnant, and both males and females were interviewed. They were recruited from two public schools in a small town in California and were interviewed in school. Respondents were between the ages of 12.25 and 18.50 years of age, with a mean age of 15.4 years; 21 of the adolescents were males and 25 were females.

Adolescents responded to a hypothetical dilemma about abortion, adapted from Gilligan et al. (1971). This dilemma concerns a teenage couple who have unprotected intercourse and face an unplanned pregnancy. Respondents are asked what they think the couple should do and the reasons for their judgments.

Hypothetical abortion dilemma: A couple about your age have been going steady for quite a while. They become more and more intimate, until finally one night they have intercourse. A few weeks later the girl finds out she is pregnant.

1. When a girl gets pregnant and doesn't want to be, what do you think the right thing to do is? Why?

    a) Do you know what abortion is? What? (For respondents who do not know, the following explanation is given: When a woman is pregnant and doesn't want to be, she can have a surgical procedure to end the pregnancy.)
    b) Are there conditions that make abortion right (and wrong)? What and Why?

2. In that situation, do you think the right thing to do would be to have the baby and place it for adoption as an alternative to abortion? Why would that be the right (wrong) thing to do?

3. Does it matter when in a pregnancy a girl wants to have an abortion? Why?

    a) Is it right (or wrong) before/after that time? Why/Why not?
    b) When do you think the fetus becomes an equal human life? Why?

4. Lets say the girl decides that having an abortion is the best solution. Why is ending the life of an unborn baby different from ending any other human life? What about a child seriously defective at birth—would it be right for the doctor to let it die? Why?

5. Who should be responsible for making this decision about abortion? Why?

    a) What if a girl and her boyfriend disagree about the right thing to do?
    b) Is it important that a girl has the right to make decisions about abortion? Why/Why not? One girl said to me that taking away her right to make decisions would be like taking away her sense of self. What do you think she meant by that? Do you agree? Why/Why not?

6. What if we lived in a country where there were no laws at all about abortion. Do you think it would still be right (wrong)? Why/Why

not? Are laws about abortion like laws about, say, murder or
stealing? Why/Why not?

7. Does it matter whether or not the girl is married if she wants to
have an abortion? Why/Why not?

   a) What if her boyfriend offers to marry her—should that make a
   difference in her decision?
   b) What if a woman just doesn't want to have children now or at
   all? Does that make a difference? Why/Why not? Does it
   matter whether or not the couple was using birth control and
   really didn't want to get pregnant?
   c) Why does that make a difference?
   d) Do you think a girl who doesn't want to have a baby should
   have sex at all? Why/Why not?

Thus, respondents are asked to reason about the rightness or wrongness of abortion, the importance of personal choice and autonomy in
decision making, the definition of human life, and the value of life.
In addition, respondents are asked about the role of significant others
in decision making, the necessity for laws regarding abortion, and
the relationship of sexual mores to abortion decisions. The interviews were scored for domain and then for developmental level within
the moral and personal domains. Agreement between two raters in
scoring half the protocols was 91 percent.

Adolescents also responded to two of Nucci's (1977) hypothetical
personal dilemmas. One of these dilemmas concerns a club rule allowing members to read other members' mail and listen in on their
phone calls. The second dilemma concerns a school rule regarding
hair length. The two dilemmas assess three aspects of thinking
within the personal domain: personal appearance, psychological concepts (concepts of self and personality), and privacy. These three
aspects were scored independently employing the descriptions contained in Nucci (1977). Agreement between two raters scoring 75
percent of the protocols was 66 percent for the personal appearance
aspect, 80 percent for psychological concepts, and 91 percent for the
privacy issues. Over 90 percent of individuals' responses for all
three aspects were at the same or adjacent level. Scores on the three
aspects were averaged to obtain one score reflecting the developmental
level of thinking within the personal domain. The modal response to
the hypothetical dilemmas was level 3 in Nucci's (1977) five-level
scheme, and responses ranged from level 1 to level 5.

In addition, adolescents were given two hypothetical moral judgment dilemmas,[1] contained in Appendix D, that probed issues of life,
law, morality, and conscience. A dilemma about overpopulation,
which will be discussed in greater detail later in the chapter, was also

included. Adolescents thus responded to a total of six hypothetical dilemmas.

DESCRIPTIONS OF REASONING

Questions concerning social conventions about sexuality and birth control and the relationships of these issues to decisions about unwanted pregnancy were included in these interviews.

Social Conventions regarding Sex and Birth Control

Characteristically, these primarily white middle-class adolescents were permissive about sexual relationships among their peers. This permissiveness was accompanied by an emphasis upon the responsible use of birth control. Fear of pregnancy was almost uniformly rejected as a valid reason for not engaging in sexual relationships, although some viewed abortion as less justified in cases where contraception was not employed. The responses below are characteristic of interviewed adolescents' reasoning regarding sexuality and birth control. Kathy and Val, both older adolescents, assert that sex is a means of personal expression.

Q. Do you think that a girl who doesn't want to have a baby should have sex at all?

A. Yeah. That's her right to. I don't think she should be deprived of sex because she doesn't want to have a child.

Q. Does it matter whether or not the couple was using birth control?

A. I think they have a certain responsibility to think about whether or not they actually want to get pregnant. [Kathy, age 17]

Q. Do you think that a girl who doesn't want to have a baby should have sex at all?

A. Yes, because it seems to me that it's an expression of lust—giving yourself—and it doesn't seem to me that the main purpose of it is to make babies. It [abortion] seems only justifiable if they were using birth control. They were making an attempt at least. It's better than some people. [Val, age 17]

A. Well, it does matter [whether or not she used birth
control]. She should have been more careful if she
really didn't want a child. She can [have sex] but she
should have something to prevent it [a pregnancy].
It's up to her because she can still get pregnant and
she has to be willing to take that chance. [Joyce,
age 15]

Sheri agrees that adolescents may engage in sexual relations
for their own pleasure. She also maintains that another valid reason
for engaging in sex is to demonstrate affection for a boyfriend.

A. If she's thought about not having a baby, maybe like
it's just for her own pleasure to do this or this is the
only way that she can really show her boyfriend how
much she loves him.

Q. So is it OK for her to have sex then in some situations, even though she doesn't want a baby?

A. Yeah. But if she doesn't want to have a baby, then
she would have done something about it like going
down and getting an IUD or getting on the pills.
[Sheri, age 15]

Some, like Josh, quoted below, express uncertainty about the
need for sex prior to marriage. He asserts that relationships take
time to develop, and that adolescents who engage in sex in the early
stages of a relationship are responding to conventional expectations,
or social pressure, rather than love. His views of sexual relationships in adolescence conform to traditional sex-role stereotypes; he
asserts that males place pressure on women to have sex and that females respond regardless of their needs.

A. If she's really into sex she can find other ways of
satisfying her needs but just stay away from the intercourse because that's what's going to get her, and
it's changed so much, like when my mom was a little
kid and now. It's like back then you waited until you
got married and it was a special thing. Some girls,
they walk around and say I've been going out with so-
and-so for three months now and we are going to bed.
Three months—you can't even develop a love relationship in three months. It takes time for a real relationship to grow and that's not going to help build it.
It's always the guys that are pressuring for it and the

girl doesn't need it. The guy maybe does. Doing
that, it's just inviting—it's a hazard. [Josh, age 17]

While others indicate that sex is permissible when birth control
is employed, their knowledge of contraception is incomplete or lacking. This is evident in the following 13-year-old male's response.

Q. Do you think that a girl who doesn't want to have a
baby should have sex at all?

A. Yeah, if she wants to, because there is birth control. We learned about it in Sex Ed. last year, but
I was so bored that I didn't really learn it. [Paul,
age 13]

Although most adolescents have obtained factual knowledge
about reproduction and contraception, this information is assimilated
and transformed to the logic of their thinking. For some, as with the
following 13-year-old female, factual information may be misconstrued.

A. Well, she can [have sex] if she wants but it depends
on your timing really.

Q. Is it wrong for her to have sex if she knows she
doesn't want to have a baby?

A. No.

Q. Why?

A. It depends really on her timing. Like certain times
you can be able to have a baby but certain times you
wouldn't. I think it's every 28 days you have your
oval or whatever and then between those 14 days you
can't but in a certain time period then that's when
you can't have a baby, but if they did it when they
couldn't have a baby then it wouldn't be wrong.
[Denise, age 13]

Although respondents differ as to when they think sex is justified
or appropriate in a relationship, most believe that not wanting a baby
is an inadequate reason for abstaining from sexual relations. Almost
all respondents state that it is wrong not to use birth control when
conception is unwanted. These responses also indicate that some
adolescents' knowledge of reproduction is vague or inadequate despite
the comprehensive sex education programs available in their schools.

Abortion may be seen as less justified when no precautions are taken to avoid a pregnancy.

Personal Reasoning

Personal responses to the abortion question, which comprised 30 percent of the sample, are consistent with the characteristics of personal judgments described in the previous chapters. Respondents believe the fetus to become a human life at birth, when it is physically separated from the mother. Abortion decisions are viewed as personal issues entailing autonomy, choice, and self-maintenance.

Differences in organization of judgments within the personal domain are described below. Responses that could be scored for developmental level in the personal domain consisted primarily of psychological concepts regarding the importance of decision making to the self.[2] Reasoning ranged from level 2 to level 4 in Nucci's (1977) five-level scheme. The modal response to the abortion interview, as well as to the hypothetical personal dilemmas, was level 3. Overall, 29 percent of respondents' personal judgments about abortion were at level 2, 10 percent were in transition between levels 2 and 3, 38 percent were at level 3, 5 percent were in transition between levels 3 and 4, and 14 percent were at level 4. Developmental differences in personal reasoning regarding abortion are discussed below.

At level 2, personal concerns focus upon the development of a personal style, the attainment of positive social status, and the avoidance of embarrassment. Personal actions may be concretely described in terms of their effect upon the body; the arena of personal actions is the self's activities and behaviors. The following adolescent male is concerned with the effects of abortion upon the woman's body. His reasoning also indicates a concern with social status; if she has an abortion early in the pregnancy no one need know of her condition. As is characteristic of personal reasoning, he maintains that the fetus becomes a life at birth.

A. When the baby is inside, it is still part of the mother, and she has the right to have an abortion. She should be able to do it any time in the pregnancy, but it would be better for both her, and her parents too if she is very young, if she has an abortion in the earlier stages so she doesn't have to go on with discomforts like morning sickness. If she has the abortion right away, if she knows that she doesn't want the baby, that would be better for her. She wouldn't suffer as much pain,

and she wouldn't have the embarrassment because
people could tell. [Mark, age 12]

His reasoning is echoed by another 12-year-old female. She is also
concerned with the avoidance of embarrassment and the maintenance
of public appearance.

A. She may be embarrassed 'cause she has to tell someone that she is pregnant 'cause there is no way she
can keep it in. [Judy, age 12]

The primary concern at the next level is the establishment and
maintenance of individuality, although individuality is defined as dif-
ferentiating oneself from the group. The subjective, psychological
self first becomes evident at this level, and respondents maintain
that the lack of opportunity to exercise choice over personal actions
results in changes in personality or a loss of individuality. This is
illustrated in the following 13-year-old's response to the abortion
dilemma. She maintains that continuing a pregnancy would change
the woman's personality.

A. [Abortion would be right] because she is young, and it
would probably wreck her life, because when you have
a child when you are young, you can't keep going to
school like you normally would. It would be so hard
to just go on with her normal type of living and better
herself. Also, if she had an abortion, she could just
not let people know. If she carried the baby, everyone would know about it, and it could change her personality somehow; she could maybe go against people
because they would talk about her having the baby and
everything. People would just look at her in a jerky
way and make her feel bad, and her parents would
probably give her a bad time. They might not understand, and make her feel ashamed of herself. If you
feel ashamed of yourself, you could go out on other
people, and you change. If she carried it long, she
would change. It [the fetus] really doesn't have a personality yet, it is just a blah. Everything starts when
it is born and is a regular human life. [Pam, age 13]

This respondent employs level 3 personal concepts not only in discussing the importance of decision making but also in discussing the
criteria for defining human life. She states that the unborn is not a
full human life because it does not possess a personality until birth.

For level 4 respondents, the self is split between the external personality and internal self, and decision making becomes a way of constantly maintaining and expressing the self. Thus, decision making about unwanted pregnancy is an important act of self-affirmation. Consciousness as a criterion for defining the unborn as a life first appears among adolescents at this level. The incidence of level 4 in this sample is low, as this level is usually achieved in late adolescence. In the example below, a 17-year-old male defines human life in terms of consciousness and briefly discusses the importance of pregnancy decision making in maintaining the self.

A. I don't think of a couple-of-months-old embryo as really having a consciousness, so I really don't think it could be called murder; I think it's silly when people go on like that. It's alive but it's not an animal or person really yet. It's like pulling up a weed in your garden. It's a personal thing. I don't think that through most of the pregnancy the unborn child really enters into it. I don't think it's anyone else's business really besides her own, because what you decide is going to affect you and what kind of person you are. What yourself is affects what decisions you make.
[Ron, age 17]

Ron distinguishes between human life and the life of the fetus through the analogy he draws between plucking a weed and terminating a pregnancy. Like other personal reasoners, Ron maintains that while the fetus is alive, it is not yet a full human life to be considered in the decision. Thus, he views abortion as an act of concern only to the individual and maintains that making personal decisions is essential to the formation of the self.

During early adolescence the personal issues of abortion concern the physical impact of abortion upon the body. Unwanted pregnancy is treated as a potentially embarrassing occurrence that might jeopardize one's social status, and therefore an important motivation for seeking abortion is to ensure that others do not become aware of one's condition. Developmental transformations in mid- and late-adolescence result in adolescents' judgments that the process of decision making about personal issues such as abortion results in the expression of the inner subjectivity of the self. Higher level reasoning within the personal domain also entails a recognition of the importance of individual choice.

Moral Reasoning

    Moral responses to the hypothetical abortion dilemma, which constituted 30 percent of the sample, are structured by justice regarding the issue of life. Moral reasoning about abortion, for adolescents treating abortion as a moral or coordinated issue, was structured at stages 2 and 3. While the moral issues of abortion are the same as those described in the previous chapters, responses are primarily at the lower stage of moral development. No principled moral reasoning in judgments about abortion or standardized moral judgment dilemmas was observed. Of the respondents who treated abortion as a moral issue, 30 percent were at stage 2, 14 percent were in transition between stages 2 and 3, 50 percent were at stage 3, and only 7 percent were at stage 4. The modal response to both the hypothetical abortion dilemma and the standardized hypothetical dilemmas was stage 3. Responses characterizing different levels of moral development are illustrated only briefly below, as they are consistent with the reasoning described in previous chapters.

    Stage 2 moral reasoning, the lowest level of reasoning observed among these adolescents, typically focuses upon the potential abuse and mistreatment of unwanted babies. This concern leads both to justifications for and against abortion. The response below is typical of reasoning at this stage. Susan asserts that both alternatives, abortion and adoption, are wrong. Rather than express a moral choice, she states that the solution is to avoid pregnancy.

> A. Well, abortion is a hard thing to do because if she wants to have a baby and she doesn't want it, she could put it in an adoption home, but that is a super hard life—to live with adoptive parents. It's almost like cold-blooded murder, though, if she gets an abortion, 'cause they are killing something. There is no real answer. If I was in that case, I wouldn't get like that. If it dies, it wouldn't have to be brought up in an adoption home or in an unpleasant home. I don't know [what's better] because I am against both of them. They are both bad. [Susan, age 12]

    The following respondent recapitulates these concerns but also begins to evaluate abortion on the basis of the emotions involved. Elements of both stage 2 and stage 3 are evident in her reasoning.

> A. [It's better to [have an abortion] than to bring an unwanted child into this world.] It's just going to probably be kicked around, put in a foster home, and

probably have a real bad life. It's better to have her
have an abortion than have her have the child and have
it unwanted. Why bring it into the world if it's just
going to be abused? It's just going to live a bad life.

Q. [When asked about laws]

A. Like if a lady wants an abortion she shouldn't be put
to the electric chair—not the death penalty. I don't
even think anything should happen to her, because it's
hers. I'm sure that if I had an abortion, I'd have one
of the worst feelings in the world, if I'd known that I
had an abortion and killed somebody—killed a baby.
[Debbie, age 15]

The right and wrong of abortion for those at moral stage 3 is
based on the feelings and social consensus of significant others.
Right action is that which gains others' approval or which is motivated
by "good" intentions. The following 15-year-old female treats abortion as a stage 3 moral issue.

Q. What do you think is the right thing to do?

A. Tell her mom. That is what I would do, 'cause her
mom and her together could probably figure it out.
I wouldn't really know what to do, that's why I'd talk
to my mom, because she could help me find out what
to do, like maybe put it up for adoption 'cause lots of
mothers want babies just born. I wouldn't have an
abortion or anything, that wouldn't be the right thing
to do. I just don't like killing off babies. Sometimes
it may be absolutely necessary, and you would absolutely have to, but I wouldn't. It's like killing off
another life. [Lisa, age 15]

Young adolescents evaluate right action as that which is most
instrumental to the mother's or fetus's needs. Concern is with the
abuse and mistreatment of unwanted babies, which may lead to moral
justifications for abortion. Moral precepts are transformed during
mid- and late-adolescence to reflect the wider social perspective of
significant others. The feelings involved become an important criterion in evaluating behavior. There is also a greater appreciation
of intentions and motivations in moral choice and behavior. This
stage 3 orientation is the modal response of adolescents in this
sample.

Coordinated Reasoning

Of the 46 interviewed adolescents, 26 percent treated abortion as a coordinated issue. The transition between domains occurs midway during the pregnancy when the fetus is defined as a human life. Judgments within both the moral and personal domains are at the lower levels of developmental maturity. The mean personal response is at level 3 in Nucci's (1977) five-level scheme, and the mean moral response is at stage 3. Respondents who consider abortion a successively personal and then moral issue coordinate concepts in the two domains by their definition of life, which is almost uniformly defined as the fetus's physical development and resemblance to human form. Adolescents are very concrete in describing the transition from personal to moral concern. As is demonstrated in the following examples, adolescents' coordinated judgments about abortion entail vivid descriptions of the stages of fetal development that differentiate personal and moral judgments.

A. If you kill it before it's born and it's early, I don't think they should do it like just before it's born and it's starting to get its brains and it's all perfect like a little baby, but if it's just getting formed and it's not totally a baby yet, maybe.

Q. [Why is it maybe OK earlier but not later?]

A. Because then you are killing something that's still being formed, but then it's made and it's all the way formed; it's just sitting there waiting to come out.

Q. When do you think it becomes an equal human life?

A. When it starts getting formed—at about six months. When it's not formed it's just a little spermy thing. [Greg, age 13]

A. Because she should hurry up and make up her mind and know what she wants instead of waiting. Because the kid is having time to grow, and then his heart starts beating, and it's starting to live, and then I don't know, to me it would get harder to get rid of.

Q. [Why?]

A. The fact that it's living more like a human. You're killing a person since it's already had time to grow. [Sheri, age 15]

A. It is a person, she would just be killing a human person if she had an abortion. Yeah, it would be, it would be manslaughter after so many months, because it is human, it has a heart, it has feet, it has legs, everything—a brain.

Q. [How about before that time?]

A. It is just a blob. It's not a person because it is not fully developed yet. It doesn't have the important parts yet. You would only be killing a blob. [Penny, age 12]

The following teen's use of a spiritual criterion in defining the unborn as a human life is unusual among this sample.

A. There's a lot of people like the right-to-life people who say the baby is alive [at conception] but I think that's still debatable in medical science. At that time, in the first three months, I think the baby does not really have a soul. It seems to me that it is just a physical thing. It's really a matter of when this baby has a soul. [Ian, age 16]

Thus, adolescents coordinate responses in the two domains by their definition of human life as full fetal development, which is described in concrete and vivid detail. Consistent with responses to hypothetical moral and personal dilemmas, responses in each domain are at the lower levels of developmental maturity.

Uncoordinated Reasoning

Confusions in reasoning about abortion would be expected among those who are either unfamiliar with the dilemma or for whom the dilemma is of low salience. As this potentially characterizes both males and young adolescents, greater frequencies of uncoordinated reasoning might be expected among these groups. However, all adolescents had participated in discussions of abortion in a progressive sex education program instituted in their schools. Therefore, all had some exposure to the issue, and the incidence of uncoordinated reasoning was low—only 13 percent of the sample (9.5 percent of those under 15 years of age and 4 percent of those over 15 years of age) expressed confusion in making judgments about abortion; this form of reasoning, where evident, was found only among males. Although exposed to the issue, these males were still confused in their thinking about abortion, and they perceived the issue to have little relevance to them. Their reasoning was marked by equivocation and confusion.

As is illustrated below, respondents were equivocal in making judgments about abortion. They attributed this to their lack of knowledge of the issue. The criteria they employed to evaluate the rightness or wrongness of abortion were inconsistent.

> <u>A.</u>   I don't know, I really don't have any idea about that because when we were learning about this I never paid much attention. I never really learned about the different stages in it so I really don't have any idea. I really don't think abortion is that OK, but I really don't know what to say. I'm so confused about it and I can't think. Other people's opinions [would be good to know] because they are the ones who really affect you more than reading. [Nick, age 15]

As was characteristic of the uncoordinated reasoning observed in this sample, Nick, a 15-year-old male, felt that his knowledge and awareness were insufficient to make judgments about abortion. Although he had been exposed to the issue of abortion, he had not assimilated the information presented in school, nor had he constructed his own opinions regarding it. Conflict, the other form of uncoordinated reasoning observed in the real-life context of decision making, was not observed at all in adolescents' responses to the hypothetical abortion dilemma.

STATISTICAL ANALYSES OF REASONING

The sample was equally divided into two age groups for statistical comparison purposes. Younger adolescents were defined as those between the ages of 12.25 and 15.19, with a mean age of 13.70. Older adolescents were defined as those between the ages of 15.21 and 18.5. Their mean age was 16.21. Comparisons of these two age groups using chi-square analyses revealed no differences in their conceptualizations of abortion. Younger and older adolescents did not differ in their use of personal, moral, coordinated, or uncoordinated concepts in reasoning about abortion. There were also no significant sex differences in reasoning about abortion.

The findings presented thus far indicate that adolescents have different modes of conceptualizing abortion and that differences in domain of judgment are not sex- or age-related. Both personal and moral interpretations of abortion are found in early adolescence.

However, there are developmental differences in the organization of judgments about abortion within the personal and moral domains, and these are moderately correlated with adolescents' reasonings about other hypothetical moral and personal issues ($r = .44$, $p < .05$ for personal judgments about the abortion and other hypothetical personal dilemmas; $r = .40$, $p < .07$ for moral reasoning about abortion and other hypothetical moral dilemmas). (These correlations are lower than the correlations reported previously between hypothetical and real-life reasoning because of the small numbers of respondents upon which each correlation is based.) Differences in the level of reasoning about abortion within the moral and personal domains are also highly age-related; age and level of personal reasoning about abortion are correlated 0.63 ($p < .0001$), and age and level of moral reasoning about abortion are correlated 0.40 ($p < .01$).

What accounts for the individual differences observed in modes of reasoning about abortion? This question is addressed in the remainder of the chapter through analyses of reasoning and demographic correlates of reasoning about abortion.

CORRELATES OF REASONING ABOUT ABORTION

A second multifaceted dilemma that could potentially be constructed within either the personal or moral domain was developed to determine whether the abortion responses were particular to this issue or whether there was consistency in adolescents' reasoning about abortion and another coordinated dilemma. The overpopulation dilemma was constructed as an analogue to abortion in terms of the moral and personal issues involved. Like abortion, this dilemma can be constructed as a personal or moral issue. The story concerns a couple's decision whether or not to have a child under conditions of overpopulation. In this dilemma, the importance of the personal choice to have a child conflicts with the needs of other family members and the wider society under conditions of scarce resources.

Hypothetical overpopulation dilemma: Mary and John have been married for several years. They are thinking about having a child, but they live in a society where there is a population problem. That is, there are too many people and not enough food or space. They already have two children, and now they can't decide whether or not to have another child.

1. What do you think they should do? Why?

2. Does it matter whether or not they have enough food or money to take care of three children? Why/Why not?

3. Mary says it's a personal decision, and that everybody should be able to make those kinds of decisions for themselves. What do you think she meant by that? Do you think that having children is a personal decision? When is it not? What other kinds of decisions would you consider personal decisions?

    a) Mary also says that part of life is being able to do what you want. Do you think she is right in this case?
    b) When do you think it's not right to do what you want?

4. Do you think they have a responsibility not to have a child?

    a) What does that mean to their family? To the community? Why?

5. Would it be fair if there was a rule that said that people couldn't have more than two children? Why/Why not? How about in these circumstances?

6. Another person said that no one can tell you what to do with your body and that, therefore, Mary should be able to decide whether or not to have another baby. Do you agree with that? Does that make a difference in this case?

The semistructured clinical interview probes the personal and moral issues of this dilemma. Either decision, to have or not have the child can result from personal or moral considerations; of importance here is the way respondents justify their conclusions. As with the abortion dilemma, domain of reasoning is determined by the structure of judgments; initially expressed decisions regarding the correct behavioral choice are treated as content. Those who treat the dilemma as a personal issue maintain that having a child should be an individual choice, that governmental rules and regulations would be an infringement of individuality and/or personal freedom, and that decisions to bear a child are private or personal matters. Those who treat the dilemma as a moral choice reason about justice or welfare issues. For some, these concerns remain unreconciled or uncoordinated. Other respondents clearly delineate the conditions under which the choice would be either a personal or moral concern; these were treated as coordinated responses. Agreement between two raters in scoring 60 percent of the interviews was 70 percent.

As with the abortion dilemma, the type of reasoning employed was not age-related. Overall, 30 percent of the adolescents treated the overpopulation dilemma as a moral choice, 41 percent treated it as a personal dilemma, 9 percent coordinated concerns in the two domains, and for 20 percent of the sample, responses were uncoordinated.

Adolescent thinking about the population dilemma was highly related to thinking about abortion ($p < .005$, contingency coefficient). Over half of the responses to the two dilemmas were the same, suggesting that adolescents' modes of response to the abortion dilemma could be generalized beyond this particular issue. The high degree of correspondence observed in responses to the two dilemmas may reflect the degree of similarity in the personal and moral issues involved.

Analyses were also conducted to determine whether different modes of conceptualizing abortion were related to either demographic variables, such as religious background and socioeconomic status, or level of reasoning about standardized hypothetical moral and personal dilemmas. Multiple discriminant analysis (Kerlinger and Pedhazur 1973) was employed to examine the strength of reasoning and demographic variables in discriminating between different modes of reasoning about abortion. Age and sex were not included, as previous analyses indicated that neither variable was significantly related to type of judgment about abortion. Developmental level in the moral and personal domains, mother's educational attainment, religious background (scored as Catholic versus all else), religious attendance, and father's occupation were included in the analysis.

Two variables, religious attendance and religious background, had the most powerful effect in predicting adolescent reasoning about abortion. The inclusion of these two variables alone accounted for 70 percent of the variance in type of judgment. Posthoc tests indicated that Catholics were more likely to consider abortion a moral issue ($p < .01$), while Protestants or those professing other religious affiliations were more likely to consider abortion a coordinated or personal issue ($p < .001$). Moral reasoners attended church more frequently than coordinated reasoners ($p < .02$) and personal reasoners ($p < .001$), although the frequency of attendance, even for moral reasoners, was quite low. The remaining variables, including socioeconomic status, as indexed by mother's education and father's occupation, and level of reasoning about hypothetical moral or personal dilemmas, had little discriminating power in predicting adolescents' judgments about abortion. These findings are consistent with the findings from the decision-making study reported in Chapter 4. That is, religious background and religiosity appear to be important factors in individuals' categorization of abortion as a moral or personal issue.

The findings presented in this chapter indicate that adolescents, like young adults, categorize abortion as a moral, personal, coordinated, or uncoordinated issue. Differences in the type of social knowledge that structures reasoning about abortion do not appear to be age- or sex-related. However, there are qualitative differences in personal and moral judgments that are related to the way adolescents structure other hypothetical moral and personal issues. Adolescent thinking about abortion must therefore be considered within the more general context of adolescents' judgments about the social world.

Adolescents' judgments about abortion are also consistent in their treatment of a second coordinated dilemma concerning overpopulation. This dilemma was administered to examine the consistency between responses regarding abortion and responses regarding another issue entailing moral issues of life and issues of personal choice. Further research must examine whether the high consistency found here in reasoning about the two dilemmas is maintained when individuals confront other issues that overlap or coordinate other aspects of the moral and personal domains.

The construction of abortion as a personal or moral issue is also related to respondents' religious backgrounds and religiosity. Catholics and those who are more religious (defined here by religious attendance) are more likely to construct abortion within the moral domain. Others were more likely to consider this dilemma a personal issue. While religious preference and religiosity differentiate adolescents' considerations of abortion as a moral or personal issue, the internalization of parental or religious values does not in itself provide a sufficient explanation of differences in adolescent judgments regarding this issue. Differences in adolescents' moral and personal judgments about abortion can be described in terms of the logic of adolescent thinking. This reflects the active, constructive, and self-regulated processes that govern the development of social knowledge.

NOTES

1. Two hypothetical moral judgment dilemmas, Story III and Story III', Form A (Kohlberg et al. 1976) were administered. These were scored for reasoning regarding the issues of life, law, morality, and conscience. Responses were scored independently by a trained scorer.

2. It should be noted that scoring of the developmental level of responses in the personal domain was based on a subset of personal responses. The majority of personal responses dealt with the criteria that respondents employed to classify abortion as a personal issue, and these were not scored for developmental level. Approximately one-third of the responses identified as personal judgments entailed scorable judgments regarding the importance of decision making to the self; these form the basis of the developmental analyses reported here.

7

CONCLUSIONS

The studies reported in this book illustrate the continuity between the way adolescents and young adults conceptualize the social
world and their reasoning about abortion. Moral, social-conventional, and personal concepts are each distinct and irreducible modes
of thought that usually pertain to different aspects of the social world.
As the studies described here indicate, although they are complexly
interwoven in judgments about abortion, they can be distinguished.
The studies also indicate that individuals use the same modes of
thinking to structure abortion and other issues within each domain.

The complexity of the abortion question arises from a fundamental disagreement as to whether or not the fetus is a human life to
be considered in the decision and, therefore, whether personal or
moral considerations should apply. While human life is usually distinguished from other forms of life in making moral judgments, the
ambiguity of abortion is that the appropriate criterion for such a judgment is unclear. For those who consider abortion a moral issue, the
genetic or spiritual potential of the fetus is enough to consider it a
human life of equal value to other living persons. For those who treat
abortion as a personal issue, the physical separation of the child from
the mother at birth marks the distinction between a person and a
lesser form of life. Once the fetus is not considered a person, social
and moral considerations are not seen to apply.

The dilemma of when to treat the fetus as a human life is not
restricted to women in the decision-making context; it also underlies
the public abortion debate. When should society exert control over
a woman's body, reproductive choices, and autonomous decision making? How broadly should society define its control over the individual?
Stated in this way, abortion raises fundamental questions about society's rights versus the rights of a person, or what shall constitute

justifiable societal regulation. The abortion debate thus entails a conflict between self and society and the limits of personal control.

The findings suggest that proponents of the so-called pro-life versus pro-choice positions are arguing fundamentally different issues that have their source in different systems of social knowledge. If compromise is to be achieved, it must be over issues that are more resolvable than whether or not the unborn fetus is a human life. The difficulty that scientists, doctors, lawyers, and other professionals concerned with the abortion issue have in rendering judgments about the personhood of the fetus is based on an acknowledgment of the ramifications of such a judgment, and the broader moral, social, and juridicial issues it raises. It is clear, however, that these are the issues that a satisfactory resolution to the abortion dilemma must address.

The findings presented here on abortion also have theoretical and methodological implications for the study of moral judgment and moral action. The issues that should be considered within a theory of morality have been debated by moral philosophers and, more recently, psychologists interested in the acquisition of moral judgment. Previous conceptions of morality, such as those employed by Kohlberg, have defined morality broadly to include such diverse considerations as sexual relations, romantic love, authority, contract, law, life, conscience, honesty, and religion. The studies presented here suggest that such global definitions of morality must be more carefully reconsidered.

There is a need for a more circumscribed definition of morality as justice that applies to a relatively limited range of issues, including the value of life, psychological or physical harm (or benefit) to others, responsibility, and the sharing of goods. Recent research describing young children's concepts of distributive (Damon 1975; DeMersseman 1976; Piaget 1948) and retributive (Irwin and Moore 1971; Piaget 1932) justice exemplifies this more limited approach and must be expanded to describe moral development across a broader age range.

When morality is more narrowly defined as justice, as was done in the studies on abortion described here, general modes of responding to moral problems do become evident. Adolescents and young adults employ the same conceptions of self and morality when reasoning about the real-life dilemma of abortion as they do in reasoning about other hypothetical moral and personal problems. This is consistent with the principles guiding these studies, which postulate that there should be a basic organization or structuring to morality, although there may be diversity in moral behavior. That is, there is a basic coherence or unity in the way individuals at any given stage structure different moral problems. That this consistency has been

lacking in other studies of moral judgment may be the result of confusions in the definition of the moral domain.

The findings on abortion should not be taken to indicate that
events themselves may be considered as moral, social-conventional,
and personal. Rather, the findings indicate that individuals share
common criteria for interpreting social events; but, as is illustrated
with abortion, the interpretation of particular actions or events as
content for the domains may vary. All individuals agree that moral
judgments involve justice or fairness. Agreement about which events
entail moral considerations should be obtained even across cultures,
as moral judgments are based upon the intrinsic features of actions,
such as the harm inflicted upon others, others' rights or well-being,
or the fair distribution of goods. In contrast, the set of actions considered to be within the personal domain and to be private and governed exclusively by the person may be more variable, as societies
may differ in the behaviors perceived to be solely personal prerogatives. As is the case with abortion, disagreements may occur when
societies define their control more extensively than some individuals
would prefer.

In addition, the conceptualization of a particular issue may
change over time. Historical analyses of legislation regarding abortion reveal that earlier legislation prohibiting abortion, repealed by
the 1973 Roe v. Wade Supreme Court decision ensuring women's constitutional right to abortion, was initially instituted to safeguard wom-
en's health and well-being. The controversy raised about abortion
as a moral issue of life and the concern with protecting the life of
the fetus is historically a relatively recent development (Mohr 1978).
Thus, abortion as a social issue has become "moralized."

While there may be few analogues to the abortion dilemma regarding ambiguities concerning the issue of life, there are many other
issues or events that cannot be clearly interpreted as content for only
one domain because they are multifaceted and overlap more than one
domain. Judgments about complex or ambiguous events may entail
the coordination or integration of concepts in different domains, either
in conflict or in synchrony with one another. The findings reported
here on relationships between judgments and actions indicate the importance of distinguishing these different interpretations for understanding the coordination of thought and action.

On a more applied note, the findings reported here on abortion
underscore the plurality of belief regarding the "rightness" or
"wrongness" of abortion. In sampling public opinion on abortion, it
is important to obtain the underlying bases for individuals' favorable
or unfavorable attitudes toward abortion. Disapproval of abortion
arising from the perceived medical risks to the woman or the inade-
quacy of current health care differs qualitatively from the belief that

abortion is taking a life. As these different concerns lead to different social policy recommendations, they require more careful consideration.

Finally, the differences described in reasoning about abortion
have implications for the provision of counseling and education for
women at risk for unwanted pregnancy. Counselors and service pro-
viders must be sensitive to the qualitatively different meanings
ascribed to abortion and to the relationship between these judgments
and the choices women make to resolve their unplanned pregnancies.
To be most effective, counseling should focus upon the domain-appropriate concerns that characterize the woman's thinking. While a focus
upon the issues foremost to the client is always consistent with good
counseling technique, it is especially important to underscore here.
Moral and personal concepts entail mutually exclusive ways of thinking about abortion. As individuals have difficulty in understanding or
respecting perspectives differing from their own, counselors must
be willing to forsake their own conceptions and adequately explore the
concerns most salient to their clients. Awareness of the issues that
structure a client's reasoning provides no simple answers as to the
"right" choice in any given unwanted pregnancy. However, the responses described in these studies do reflect normative concerns expressed by different women and, therefore, the potentially most fruit-
ful issues to pursue in a counseling session. The interviews also
demonstrate that the more sensitive issues of abortion may be asked
with no negative effect, either in changing women's intentions to have
an abortion or in their responses to the abortion experience.

In addition to considering the different meanings ascribed to
abortion, those directly concerned with providing education or service
must consider developmental differences in the way individuals structure moral and personal issues. Researchers have identified the
structure of messages that individuals at given developmental stages
find most preferable and comprehensible (Rest, Turiel, and Kohlberg
1969). Maximum preference is given for reasoning that is slightly
more advanced than the individual's own level, but not too advanced
as to be incomprehensible. Using age norms rather than individual
data, this knowledge could be incorporated into programs on unwanted
pregnancy and birth control to help structure more effective communications. This may be particularly useful in addressing adolescent populations, currently a target of national concern.

The assertion that educational programs be constructed in accordance with developmental concerns also implies that greater atten-
tion be given to adolescents' and young adults' reasoning about these
issues. The research described herein demonstrates that providing
information regarding birth control and sexuality does not necessarily
ensure understanding, and that understanding develops through a self-

constructed, self-regulated process that entails the active assimilation of information. Educational formats that encourage active discussion and participation are more likely to facilitate this than programs that prescribe values. Adolescents must be allowed to think through the issues themselves and to discover adequate solutions to the problems presented.

Reasoning and decision making about issues such as abortion must be considered in the context of adolescents' and young adults' developing conceptions of the social world, and the conflict engendered in resolving these dilemmas can also be seen as a potential stimulus for further personal and moral growth.

APPENDIX A

DEMOGRAPHIC CHARACTERISTICS OF THE STUDY SAMPLE

	Aborters	Continuers	Never-Pregnant
Age			
Mean	20.80	20.39	20.55
Standard deviation	3.20	4.93	3.81
Education (percent)			
Completed less than 12 years	8	61	32
Completed 12 to 16 years	88	30	59
Completed more than 16 years	4	9	9
Mother's education (percent)			
Completed less than 12 years	20	57	9
Completed 12 to 16 years	48	39	64
Completed more than 16 years	32	4	27
Father's education (percent)			
Completed less than 12 years	17	46	27
Completed 12 to 16 years	29	36	50
Completed more than 16 years	54	18	23
Occupation* (percent)			
Professional	0	0	5
White collar	12	13	9
Blue collar	8	22	23
Unemployed/student	80	65	64
Mother's occupation* (percent)			
Professional	17	9	18
White collar	52	41	50
Blue collar	13	18	23
Unemployed/student	17	32	9
Father's occupation* (percent)			
Professional	39	29	20
White collar	35	33	65
Blue collar	26	33	15
Unemployed/student	0	5	0
Religious background (percent)			
Catholic	32	48	27
Protestant	28	44	36
Jewish (or other)	20	9	27
None	20	0	9
Religious attendance (percent)			
One or two times a week	0	22	0
Less than one or two times a month	8	13	5
Less than one or two times a year	24	22	27
Never	68	44	68

*As indexed by the Index of Urban Status.

Note: Percentages may not equal 100 because of rounding.

APPENDIX B

ABORTION INTERVIEW AND
HYPOTHETICAL MORAL DILEMMAS

ABORTION INTERVIEW

1. When, in general, do you think abortion should be permitted? Why?

   a. Is it wrong after that time? Why?
   b. Why is it alright before that time?

2. When in the course of its development would you say the fetus becomes a human life?

   a. What characteristics would you require to make that judgment?
   b. How does that affect your judgments of the rightness or wrongness of abortion?

3. Is abortion different from deciding at birth that a child should live? In what way?

   a. How do you weigh the child's needs versus the mother's needs in the abortion decision?

4. Do you think there should be laws about abortion? What kind? Why?

   a. Is a law about abortion the same kind of law as, say, a law about murder or stealing? Why/Why not?
   b. Do you think the government should have the right to make abortion illegal? Why/Why not?

5. Should women have the right to make decisions about abortion? Why/Why not? How would not having the right to make decisions about abortion affect your feelings of personal choice?

6. One woman said to me that taking away her right to make decisions about abortion would be like taking away her sense of self. What do you think she meant? Do you agree? Why/Why not?

7. What role should the partner play in the decision? Why?

   a. Who should decide if the woman and her partner disagree? Why?

8. Does a woman have any obligations to society to have/not have children?

   a. Do you think it is part of women's roles to have children? Should that affect her decision about this pregnancy?

143

b. Does it matter if she is unmarried? Why/Why not?
c. Does it matter what other people think a woman should do? Why/Why not?
d. Should it matter whether she has one sexual partner or not?

For pregnant respondents:

9. What was the most important reason for you to decide to have an abortion/not to have an abortion?

a. What factors were important in your decision? Why?
b. What things did you consider in your decision?
c. How do you feel about having an abortion/having the child?
d. Have your feelings changed about abortion since you found out you were pregnant?
e. Did you consider (the alternate choice)?

10. What role did your partner/parents/friends play in the decision?

HYPOTHETICAL MORAL JUDGMENT DILEMMAS

In Europe, a woman was near death from a special kind of cancer. There was one drug that the doctors thought might save her. It was a form of radium that a druggist in the same town had recently discovered. The drug was expensive to make, but the druggist was charging ten times what the drug cost him to make. He paid $200 for the radium and charged $2,000 for a small dose of the drug. The sick woman's husband, Heinz, went to everyone he knew to borrow the money, but he could only get together $1,000, which is half of what it cost. He told the druggist that his wife was dying, and asked him to sell it cheaper or let him pay later. But the druggist said, "No, I discovered the drug and I'm going to make money from it." So Heinz got desperate and broke into the man's store to steal the drug for his wife.

1. Should Heinz steal the drug? Why?
2. Which is worse, letting someone die or stealing? Why?
   a. What does the value of life mean to you, anyway?
3. Is there a good reason for a husband to steal if he doesn't love his wife?
4. Would it be as right to steal it for a stranger as for his wife? Why
5. Heinz steals the drug and is caught. Should the judge sentence him or let him go free? Why?
6. The judge thinks of letting him go free. What would be his reasons for doing so?

7. Thinking in terms of society, what would be the best reason for the judge to give him some sentence?
8. Thinking in terms of society, what would be the best reason for the judge not to give him some sentence?

In a country in Europe, a poor man named Valjean could find no work, nor could his sister or brother. Without money, he stole food and medicine that they needed. He was captured and sentenced to prison for six years. After a couple of years, he escaped from the prison and went to live in another part of the country under a new name. He saved money and slowly built up a big factory. He gave his workers the highest wages and used most of his profits to build a hospital for the people who couldn't afford good medical care. Twenty years had passed when a tailor recognized the factory owner as being Valjean, the escaped convict whom the police had been looking for back in his home town.

1. Should the tailor report Valjean to the police? Why?
2. Suppose Valjean were reported and brought before the judge. Should the judge have him finish his sentence or let him go free?
3. From society's point of view, what would be the best reason for the judge to have Valjean finish his sentence?
4. From society's point of view, what would be the best reason for the judge to let him go free?
5. The law says citizens are supposed to report escaped convicts. Could someone be considered a good citizen and not report a convict like in this case? Why?
6. What considerations should guide a good citizen in cases where there is a conflict between the law and his own judgment?

APPENDIX C

FOLLOW-UP ABORTION INTERVIEW AND HYPOTHETICAL MORAL DILEMMAS

FOLLOW-UP INTERVIEW ABOUT ABORTION

1. How have things changed since you had your abortion/your child?

2. Are you still in school/working?

3. Have you been pregnant since we last talked, and if so, how did you resolve your pregnancy?

4. How do you feel now about having had an abortion/your baby?

5. How did the experience affect your relationships with your partner/parents/friends?

6. How did having an abortion/having a child change your feelings about yourself? About your sense of competency? About your feelings of control over your life? (and the like)

7. Have your feelings about abortion changed since we talked last?

8. Would you describe having an abortion/having a child as a growth experience and in what ways?

9. What would you do now if faced with another pregnancy? Why?

10. How do you feel, more generally, now about abortion?

    a. When do you think abortion should be permissible? Why?
    b. Why is it permissible up to this point?
    c. Would it be wrong after that point and why?

11. When do you think the fetus becomes an equal human life? Why? Why is that important in your thinking about abortion?

HYPOTHETICAL MORAL JUDGMENT DILEMMAS

Heinz did break into the store. He stole the drug and gave it to his wife. In the newspapers the next day, there was an account of the robbery. Mr. Brown, a police officer who knew Heinz, read the account. He remembered seeing Heinz running away from the store and realized that it was Heinz who stole the drug. Mr. Brown wonders whether he should report that Heinz was the robber.

147

1. Should Officer Brown report Heinz for stealing? Why/Why not?
2. Officer Brown finds and arrests Heinz. Heinz is brought to court, and a jury is selected. The jury's job is to find whether a person is innocent or guilty of committing a crime. The jury finds Heinz guilty. It is up to the judge to determine the sentence. Should the judge give Heinz some sentence, or should he suspend the sentence and let Heinz go free? Why?
3. Thinking in terms of society, should people who break the law be punished? Why/Why not?
   a. How does this apply to what Heinz should do?
4. Heinz was doing what his conscience told him when he stole the drug. Should a lawbreaker be punished if he is acting out of conscience? Why/Why not?

There was a woman who had very bad cancer, and there was no treatment known to medicine that would save her. Her doctor, Dr. Jefferson, knew that she had only about six months to live. She was in terrible pain, but she was so weak that a good dose of a pain-killer like ether or morphine would make her die sooner. She was delirious and almost crazy with pain, and in her calm periods she would ask Dr. Jefferson to give her enough ether to kill her. She said she couldn't stand the pain and she was going to die in a few months anyway. Although he knows that mercy killing is against the law, the doctor thinks about granting her request.

1. Should Dr. Jefferson give her the drug that would make her die? Why/Why not?
2. Should the woman have the right to make the final decision? Why/Why not?
3. The woman is married. Should her husband have anything to do with the decision? Why/Why not?
4. Is there any way a person has a duty or obligation to live when he or she does not want to, when the person wants to commit suicide? Why/Why not?
5. It is against the law for the doctor to give the woman the drug. Does that make it morally wrong? Why/Why not?
6. Should people try to do everything they can to obey the law? Why/Why not?
   a. How does this apply to what Dr. Jefferson should do?

APPENDIX D

HYPOTHETICAL PERSONAL DILEMMAS

John, a boy about your age, wears his hair down to his should-
One day, when he came to school, his teacher called him aside
and told him that his hair was too long and that he would have to get
it cut. He told her that it was his hair and that he liked it that way.
But the teacher said, "That may be what you like, but the school has
its rules."

1. Should John cut his hair? Why/Why not?
2. If you could decide if there would be a rule saying that boys have
   to cut their hair, would you have that rule? Why/Why not?
3. John goes to the principal and tells him that he wants to grow his
   hair long so that he won't be like other boys. Should John be
   able to wear his hair different from the other boys?
4. Would it be good if all the boys had to wear their hair exactly the
   same way?
5. Do you ever do anything with your hair or your clothes to be
   special?
   a. How come?
6. Suppose the school told you that you couldn't wear your hair the
   way that you do—would that be right? Why/Why not?
   a. Would you follow that rule? (If no:) Can you give me two
      good reasons why you should be able to do what you want
      with your own hair?
7. Why is it important to be able to decide how you wear your hair?
8. A boy/girl student at another school told me that he/she likes to
   wear his/her hair the way he/she wants because it lets everybody
   know that he/she is an individual. What did he/she mean by that?
   Do you agree with him/her?
9. She/he also said that her/his hair was a way of telling people
   what kind of girl/boy she/he is. What do you think she/he meant
   by that?
10. Another boy/girl student told me that you should wear your hair
    the way you want in order to be "your self." What did he/she
    mean by that?
11. What is a self? Are your thoughts and imaginings part of your
    self?
    a. In what way?
    b. Is the way you wear your hair related to your self? How?
12. What is your personality? Is it different from your self?
    a. Is the way you keep your hair related to your personality?
    b. In what way?

Jonathan, another boy about your age, belongs to a club. One day, when he gets to the clubhouse, his friends are having a discussion. One girl says that Jonathan hasn't been following the club rules; he hasn't been letting the other club members read any of the letters he gets or listen in on his phone calls. He tells them that he doesn't have to, that his letters and phone calls are to him and nobody else. Another boy says that the club rules are that he is supposed to let them read all his letters and tell them who he talks on the phone with and what they say. He answers, "I don't care. My letters and phone calls are my business, and they are for me and nobody else."

1. Should Jonathan let the club members read his mail and listen to his phone calls? Why/Why not?
2. What are Jonathan's obligations to the club?
   a. Do they include letting people read his mail and listen to his phone calls?
3. Would you want a rule like that in your club? Why/Why not?
4. Is it important to have privacy? Why/Why not?
   a. Why do you think people need privacy?

   (If answer is in terms of protection from embarrassment:)

   b. Why would someone else finding out about a private thing be embarrassing?
   c. Is there any other reason, other than it would embarrass Jonathan that he should keep some things private?
   d. Is there any other reason than embarrassment that you would want to keep some things private?
5. Do you think Jonathan should be able to keep secrets from the other people in the club? Why/Why not?

REFERENCES

Abernathy, V. 1974. "Illegitimate Conception among Teenagers."
American Journal of Public Health 64: 662-65.

Adler, N. 1979a. "Abortion: A Psychosocial Perspective." Journal of Social Issues 35: 100-19.

_____. 1979b. "Decision Models in Population Research." Journal of Population: Behavioral, Social and Environmental Issues 2: 187-202.

_____. 1975. "Emotional Responses of Women following Therapeutic Abortion." American Journal of Orthopsychiatry 45: 446-56.

Alan Guttmacher Institute. 1976. Eleven Million Teenagers: What Can Be Done about the Epidemic of Adolescent Pregnancies in the U.S. New York: Planned Parenthood Federation of America.

Arney, W. R., and W. H. Trescher. 1976. "Trends in Attitudes toward Abortion, 1972-1975." Family Planning Perspectives 8: 117-24.

Aronfreed, J. 1968. Conduct and Conscience: The Socialization of Internalized Control over Behavior. New York: Academic Press.

Baldwin, W. 1977. "Adolescent Pregnancy and Child-bearing— Growing Concerns for Americans." Population Bulletin 31: 1-35.

Bandura, A., and F. J. McDonald. 1963. "The Influence of Social Reinforcement and the Behavior of Models in Socializing Children's Moral Judgments." Journal of Abnormal and Social Psychology 67: 274-81.

Barglow, P., M. Bornstein, D. B. Exum, M. K. Wright, and H. N. Visotsky. 1968. "Some Psychiatric Aspects of Illegitimate Pregnancy in Early Adolescence." American Journal of Orthopsychiatry 38: 672-87.

Barglow, P., and S. Weinstein. 1974. "Therapeutic Abortion during Adolescence: Psychiatric Observations." Journal of Youth and Adolescence 2: 331-42.

Belenky, M. F. 1977. "The Role of Conflict in Moral Development: Resolving the Abortion Dilemma." Mimeographed. Cambridge, Mass.: Harvard University.

Belenky, M. F., and C. Gilligan. 1979. "The Impact of Abortion Decisions on Moral Development of Adolescent and Adult Women." Paper presented at the Annual Convention of the American Psychological Association, New York.

Beswick, D. G. 1970. "Attitudes to Taking Human Life." Australia and New Zealand Journal of Sociology 6: 120-30.

Blasi, A. 1980. "Bridging Moral Cognition and Moral Action: A Critical Review of the Literature." Psychological Bulletin 88: 1-45.

Boyle, R. P. 1970. "Path Analysis and Ordinal Scale Data." American Journal of Sociology 75: 461-80.

Bracken, M. B., M. Hachamovitch, and G. Grossman. 1974. "The Decision to Abort and Psychological Sequelae." Journal of Nervous and Mental Disease 158: 154-62.

Bracken, M. B., L. V. Klerman, and M. Bracken. 1978. "Coping with Pregnancy Resolution among Never-Married Women." American Journal of Orthopsychiatry 48: 320-33.

Broughton, J. 1978. "Development of Concepts of Self, Mind, Reality, and Knowledge." In New Directions for Child Development: Social Cognition, edited by W. Damon. San Francisco: Jossey-Bass.

Buss, A. 1978. "Causes and Reasons in Attribution Theory: A Conceptual Critique." Journal of Personality and Social Psychology 36: 1311-21.

Callahan, D. 1970. Abortion: Law, Choice, and Morality. New York: Macmillan.

Cheyne, J. A. 1971. "Some Parameters of Punishment Affecting Resistance to Deviation and Generalization of a Prohibition." Child Development 42: 1249-61.

Colby, A., L. Kohlberg, and J. Gibbs. 1979. "A Longitudinal Study of Moral Judgment." Paper presented at Annual Meeting of the Society for Research in Child Development, San Francisco.

Damon, W. 1977. The Social World of the Child. San Francisco: Jossey-Bass.

_____. 1975. "Early Conceptions of Positive Justice as Related to the Development of Logical Operations." Child Development 46: 301-12.

DeMersseman, S. A. 1976. "A Developmental Investigation of Children's Moral Reasoning and Behavior in Hypothetical and Practical Situations." Ph.D. dissertation, University of California, Berkeley.

Diamond, M., P. G. Steinhoff, J. A. Palmore, and R. G. Smith. 1973. "Sexuality, Birth Control, and Abortion: A Decision-Making Sequence." Journal of Biosocial Science 5: 347-61.

Elkind, D. 1967. "Egocentrism in Adolescence." Child Development 38: 1025-34.

Erikson, E. 1968. Identity, Youth and Crisis. New York: W. W. Norton.

Evans, J. R., G. Selstad, and W. H. Welcher. 1976. "Teenagers: Fertility Control Behavior and Attitudes before and after Abortion, Childbearing or Negative Pregnancy Test." Family-Planning Perspectives 8: 192-200.

Fischman, S. 1977. "Delivery or Abortion in Inner-City Adolescents." American Journal of Orthopsychiatry 47: 121-33.

Flavell, J. H., and J. Wohlwill. 1969. "Formal and Functional Aspects of Cognitive Development." In Studies in Cognitive Development, edited by D. Elkind and J. Flavell. New York: Oxford.

Ford, C., P. Castelnuovo-Tedesco, and K. Long. 1972. "Women Who Seek Abortion: A Comparison with Women Who Complete Their Pregnancies." American Journal of Psychiatry 129: 546-52.

Freeman, E. 1977. "Influence of Personality Attributes on Abortion Experiences." American Journal of Orthopsychiatry 47: 503-13.

Freud, A. 1966. The Ego and the Mechanisms of Defense. New York: International Universities Press.

Furth, H. G. 1978. "Children's Societal Understanding and the Process of Equilibration." In New Directions for Child Development: Social Cognition, edited by W. Damon. San Francisco: Jossey-Bass.

Gibbs, J. 1979. "Kohlberg's Moral Stage Theory: A Piagetian Revision." Human Development 22: 89-112.

_____. 1977. "Kohlberg's Stages of Moral Judgment: A Constructive Critique." Harvard Educational Review 47: 43-59.

Gilligan, C. 1977. "In a Different Voice: Women's Conceptions of Self and of Morality." Harvard Educational Review 47: 481-518.

Gilligan, C., and M. Belenky. 1980. "A Naturalistic Study of Abortion Decisions." In New Directions in Child Development: Clinical-Developmental Psychology, edited by R. L. Selman and R. Yando. San Francisco: Jossey-Bass.

Gilligan, C., L. Kohlberg, J. Lerner, and M. Belenky. 1971. "Moral Reasoning about Sexual Dilemmas." In Technical Report of the Commission on Obscenity and Pornography, vol. 1, no. 5256-0010, pp. 141-74. Washington, D.C.: Government Printing Office.

Goldsmith, S., L. Potts, L. Green, and R. Miller. 1970. "Counseling and Referral for Legal Abortion in California's Bay Area." Family Planning Perspectives 2: 14-19.

Gordon, N. J. 1976. "Children's Recognition and Conceptualizations of Emotions in Videotape Presentations." Ph.D. dissertation, Harvard University.

Grim, P., L. Kohlberg, and S. White. 1968. "Some Relationships between Conscience and Attentional Processes." Journal of Personality and Social Psychology 8: 239-253.

Haan, N. 1978. "Two Moralities in Action Contexts: Relationships to Thought, Ego Regulation, and Development." Journal of Personality and Social Psychology 36: 286-305.

_____. 1975. "Hypothetical and Actual Moral Reasoning in a Situation of Civil Disobedience." Journal of Personality and Social Psychology 32: 255-70.

Haan, N., M. B. Smith, and J. Block. 1968. "Moral Reasoning of Young Adults: Political-Social Behavior, Family Background, and Personality Correlates." Journal of Personality and Social Psychology 10: 183-201.

Hatcher, S. 1973. "The Adolescent Experience of Pregnancy and Abortion: A Developmental Analysis." Journal of Youth and Adolescence 1: 53-102.

Inhelder, B., and J. Piaget. 1964. The Early Growth of Logic in the Child. New York: Harper.

_____. 1958. The Growth of Logical Thinking from Childhood to Adolescence. New York: Basic.

Irwin, D. M., and S. G. Moore. 1971. "The Young Child's Understanding of Social Justice." Developmental Psychology 5: 406-10.

Jacobsson, L., C. Perris, G. Roman, and O. Roman. 1974. "A Social-Psychiatric Comparison of 399 Women Requesting Abortion and 118 Pregnant Women Intending to Deliver." Acta Psychiatrica Scandinavica 255: 279-90.

Jones, E. F., and C. F. Westoff. 1978. "How Attitudes towards Abortion Are Changing." Journal of Population 1: 5-21.

Kagan, J. 1971. "A Conception of Early Adolescence." In 12 to 16: Early Adolescence, edited by J. Kagan and R. Coles. New York: W. W. Norton.

Kane, F., and P. Lackensbuch. 1973. "Adolescent Pregnancy: A Study of Aborters and Nonaborters." American Journal of Orthopsychiatry 43: 796-803.

Keasey, C. B. 1975. "Implicators of Cognitive Development." In Moral Development: Current Theory and Research, edited by D. J. DePalma and J. M. Foley. Hillsdale, N.J.: Erlbaum Associates.

Kerlinger, F., and E. Pedhazur. 1973. Multiple Regression in Behavioral Research. New York: Holt, Rinehart and Winston.

Knutson, A. L. 1973. "A New Human Life and Abortion: Beliefs, Ideal Values, and Value Judgments." In Psychological Perspectives on Population, edited by J. T. Fawcett. New York: Basic.

Kohlberg, L. 1976. "Moral Stages and Moralization: The Cognitive-Developmental Approach." In Moral Development and Behavior Theory, Research and Social Issues, edited by T. Lickona. New York: Holt, Rinehart and Winston.

_____. 1971. "From Is to Ought: How to Commit the Naturalistic Fallacy and Get Away with It in the Study of Moral Development." In Cognitive Development and Epistemology, edited by T. Mischel. New York: Academic Press.

_____. 1969. "Stage and Sequence: The Cognitive-Developmental Approach to Socialization." In Handbook of Socialization Theory and Research, edited by D. Goslin. New York: Rand McNally.

_____. 1958. "The Development of Modes of Moral Thinking and Choices in the Years Two to Sixteen." Ph.D. dissertation, University of Chicago.

Kohlberg, L., A. Colby, J. C. Gibbs, D. Speicher-Dubin, and C. Power. 1976. "Identifying Moral Stages: A Manual." Mimeographed. Cambridge, Mass.: Harvard University.

Kohlberg, L., and D. Elfenbein. 1975. "The Development of Moral Judgments Concerning Capital Punishment." American Journal of Orthopsychiatry 45: 614-39.

Kohlberg, L., and C. Gilligan. 1971. "The Adolescent as a Philosopher: The Discovery of the Self in a Post-Conventional World." In 12 to 16: Early Adolescence, edited by J. Kagan and R. Coles. New York: W. W. Norton.

Kohlberg, L., and R. Kramer. 1969. "Continuities and Discontinuities in Childhood and Adult Moral Development." Human Development 12: 93-120.

Kramer, R. 1968. "Moral Development in Young Adulthood." Ph.D. dissertation, University of Chicago.

Kuhn, D., J. Langer, L. Kohlberg, and N. Haan. 1977. "The Development of Formal Operations in Logical and Moral Judgment." Genetic Psychology Monographs 95: 97-188.

Langer, J. 1969. "Disequilibrium as a Source of Development."
In Trends and Issues in Developmental Psychology, edited by
P. H. Mussen, J. Langer, and M. Covington. New York:
Holt, Rinehart and Winston.

Luker, K. 1974. Taking Chances: Abortion and the Decision Not
to Contracept. Berkeley: University of California Press.

Margolis, A., L. Davison, K. Hanson, S. Loos, and C. Mikkelson.
1971. "Therapeutic Abortion: A Follow-up Study." American
Journal of Obstretrics and Gynecology 110: 243-49.

McNamee, S. M. 1977. "Moral Behavior, Moral Development, and
Motivation." Journal of Moral Education 7: 27-31.

Miller, W. B. 1973. "Psychological Vulnerability to Unwanted
Pregnancy." Family Planning Perspectives 5: 199-201.

Mohr, J. 1978. Abortion in America. New York: Oxford University Press.

Monsour, K., and B. Stewart. 1973. "Abortion and Sexual Behavior
in College Women." American Journal of Orthopsychiatry 43: 5.

Much, N., and R. Schweder. 1978. "Speaking of Rules: The Analysis of Culture in Breach." In New Directions for Child Development: Moral Development, edited by W. Damon. San
Francisco: Jossey-Bass.

National Center for Health Statistics. 1979. Natality Statistics.
Monthly Vital Statistics Report, vol. 27, suppl. 11.

Noonan, J. T., Jr., ed. 1970. The Morality of Abortion: Legal
and Historical Perspectives. Cambridge, Mass.: Harvard
University Press.

Nucci, L. 1981. "The Development of Personal Concepts: A Domain Distinct from Moral or Societal Concepts." Child Development 52: 114-21.

_____. 1977. "Social Development: Personal, Conventional and
Moral Concepts." Ph.D. dissertation, University of California, Santa Cruz.

Nucci, L., and P. Nucci. In press. "Children's Social Interactions in the Context of Moral and Conventional Transgressions." Child Development.

Nucci, L., and E. Turiel. 1978. "Social Interactions and the Development of Social Concepts in Pre-School Children." Child Development 49: 400-7.

Olson, L. 1980. "Social and Psychological Correlates of Pregnancy Resolution among Adolescent Women: A Review." American Journal of Orthopsychiatry 50: 432-45.

Oskamp, S., B. Mindick, and D. Berger. 1974. "Predicting Success Versus Failure in Contraceptive Planning." Paper presented at the American Psychological Association Convention, New Orleans.

Osofsky, J., and H. Osofsky. 1972. "The Psychological Reaction of Patients to Legalized Abortion." American Journal of Orthopsychiatry 42: 48-60.

Payne, E. C., A. R. Kravitz, M. T. Notman, and J. V. Anderson. 1976. "Outcome following Therapeutic Abortion." Archives of General Psychiatry 33: 725-33.

Peck, A., and H. Marcus. 1966. "Psychiatric Sequelae of Therapeutic Interruption of Pregnancy." Journal of Nervous and Mental Disease 143: 417-25.

Peevers, E. H., and P. F. Secord. 1973. "Developmental Changes in Attribution of Descriptive Concepts to Persons." Journal of Personality and Social Psychology 27: 120-28.

Perez-Reyes, M., and R. Falk. 1969. "Follow-up after Therapeutic Abortion in Early Adolescents." Archives of General Psychiatry 20: 408-14.

Piaget, J. 1976. The Grasp of Consciousness. Cambridge, Mass.: Harvard University Press.

_____. 1970a. "Piaget's Theory." In Carmichael's Manual of Child Psychology, edited by P. Mussen, 3d ed. New York: Wiley.

_____. 1970b. Structuralism. New York: Basic.

_____. 1967. *Six Psychological Studies*. New York: Random House.

_____. 1960. *The Child's Conception of the World*. Patterson, N.J.: Littlefield, Adams.

_____. 1950. *The Psychology of Intelligence*. New York: Harcourt, Brace.

_____. 1948. *The Moral Judgment of the Child*. Glencoe, Ill.: Free Press.

Potter, R. B., Jr. 1969. "The Abortion Debate." In *Updating Life and Death: Essays in Ethics and Medicine*, edited by D. R. Cutler. Boston: Beacon Press.

Pratt, M. A. 1975. "Developmental Study of Person Perception and Attributions of Social Causality: Learning the What and Why of Others." Ph.D. dissertation, Harvard University.

Rapoport, J. L. 1965. "American Abortion Applicants in Sweden." *Archives of General Psychiatry* 13: 24-33.

Rawls, J. 1971. *A Theory of Justice*. Cambridge, Mass.: Harvard University Press.

Rest, J., E. Turiel, and L. Kohlberg. 1969. "Level of Moral Judgment as a Determinant of Preference and Comprehension of Moral Judgments Made by Others." *Journal of Personality and Social Psychology* 37: 225-52.

Rosen, R. H., J. W. Ager, and L. J. Martindale. 1979. "Contraception, Abortion, and Self Concept." *Journal of Population: Behavioral, Social, and Environmental Issues* 2: 118-39.

Rossi, A. S. 1967. "Public Views on Abortion." In *The Case for Legalized Abortion Now*, edited by A. F. Guttmacher. Berkeley: Diablo Press.

Rothman, G. 1980. "The Relationship between Moral Judgment and Moral Behavior." In *Moral Development and Socialization*, edited by M. Windmiller, N. Lambert, and E. Turiel. Boston: Allyn and Bacon.

St. John-Stevas, N. 1963. *The Right to Life*. London: Hodder and Stoughton.

Schaeffer, C., and F. Pine. 1972. "Pregnancy, Abortion, and the Developmental Tasks of Adolescence." Journal of the American Academy of Child Psychiatry 11: 511-36.

Schur, E. M. 1965. Crimes without Victims: Deviant Behavior and Public Policy—Abortion, Homosexuality, Drug Addiction. Englewood Cliffs, N.J.: Prentice-Hall.

Schwartz, S. H., K. A. Feldman, M. E. Brown, and A. Heingartner. 1969. "Some Personality Correlates of Conduct in Two Situations of Moral Conflict." Journal of Personality 37: 41-57.

Sears, R. R., E. E. Maccoby, and H. Levin. 1957. Patterns of Child Rearing. Evanston, Ill.: Row, Peterson.

Selman, R. 1976. "Social-Cognitive Understanding: A Guide to Education and Clinical Practice." In Moral Development and Behavior: Theory, Research, and Social Issues, edited by T. Lickona. New York: Holt, Rinehart and Winston.

Shantz, C. U. 1975. "The Development of Social Cognition." In Review of Child Development Research, edited by E. M. Hetherington, vol. 5. Chicago: University of Chicago Press.

Siegel, S. 1956. Nonparametric Statistics for the Behavioral Sciences. New York: McGraw-Hill.

Simon, N., and A. Senturia. 1966. "Psychiatric Sequelae of Abortion." Archives of General Psychiatry 15: 378-89.

Simon, N., A. Senturia, and D. Rothman. 1967. "Psychiatric Illness following Therapeutic Abortion." American Journal of Psychiatry 124: 97-103.

Simon, N. M., B. A. Senturia, D. Rothman, and J. T. Goff. 1969. "Psychological Factors Related to Spontaneous and Therapeutic Abortion." American Journal of Obstetrics and Gynecology 104: 799-806.

Slaby, R. E., and R. D. Parke. 1971. "Effect on Resistance to Deviation of Observing a Model's Affective Reactions to Response Consequences." Developmental Psychology 5: 40-47.

Smetana, J. 1981. "Preschool Children's Conceptions of Moral and Social Rules." Child Development 52: 4408-11.

_____. 1980. "Prosocial Events and Transgressions in the Moral and Societal Domains." Paper presented at the annual meeting of the American Educational Research Association, Boston.

_____. 1979. "Beliefs about the Permissibility of Abortion and Their Relationship to Decisions Regarding Abortion." Journal of Population: Behavioral, Social and Environmental Issues 2: 294-305.

Smetana, J., and N. Adler. 1980. "Fishbein's Value x Expectancy Model: An Examination of Some Assumptions." Personality and Social Psychology Bulletin 6: 89-96.

_____. 1979. "Understanding the Abortion Decision: A Test of Fishbein's Expectancy x Value Model." Journal of Population: Behavioral, Social and Environmental Issues 24: 338-57.

Smetana, J., D. Bridgeman, and E. Turiel. Forthcoming. "Differentiation of Domains and Prosocial Reasoning." In The Nature of Prosocial Development: Interdisciplinary Theories and Strategies, edited by D. Bridgeman. New York: Academic Press.

Smith, E. M. 1973. "A Follow-up Study of Women who Request Abortion." American Journal of Orthopsychiatry 43: 574-85.

Stein, J. L. 1973. "Adolescent's Reasoning about Moral and Sexual Dilemmas: A Longitudinal Study." Ph.D. dissertation, Harvard University.

Steinhoff, P. G., R. G. Smith, and M. Diamond. 1972. "Characteristics and Motivations of Women Receiving Abortions." Sociological Symposium 8: 83-89.

Szasz, T. 1966. "The Ethics of Abortion." Humanist 6: 147-48.

Tangri, S. S. 1976. "A Feminist Perspective on Some Ethical Issues in Population Programs." Signs: Journal of Women in Culture and Society 1: 895-904

Turiel, E. In preparation. "A Longitudinal Analysis of Concepts of Social Convention."

_____. Forthcoming. "Domains and Categories in Social Cognition." In The Relationship between Social and Cognitive Development, edited by W. Overton.

_____. 1979. "Distinct Conceptual and Developmental Domains: Social-Convention and Morality." In Nebraska Symposium on Motivation, edited by C. B. Keasey. Lincoln: University of Nebraska Press.

_____. 1978a. "Social Regulations and Domains of Social Concepts." In New Directions for Child Development: Social Cognition, edited by W. Damon. San Francisco: Jossey-Bass.

_____. 1978b. "The Development of Concepts of Social Structure." In Personality and Social Development, edited by J. Glick and A. Clarke-Stewart, vol. 1. New York: Gardner Press.

_____. 1975. "The Development of Social Concepts: Mores, Customs and Conventions." In Moral Development: Current Theory and Research, edited by D. J. DePalma and J. M. Foley. Hillsdale, N.J.: Laurence Erlbaum Associates.

_____. 1974. "Conflict and Transition in Adolescent Moral Development." Child Development 45: 14-29.

_____. 1972. "Stage Transition in Moral Development." In Second Handbook of Research on Teaching, edited by R. M. Travers. Chicago: Rand McNally.

_____. 1969. "Developmental Process in the Child's Moral Thinking." In Trends and Issues in Developmental Psychology, edited by P. H. Mussen, J. Langer, and M. Covington. New York: Holt, Rinehart and Winston.

_____. 1966. "An Experimental Test of the Sequentiality of Developmental Stages in the Child's Moral Judgments." Journal of Personality and Social Psychology 3: 611-18.

Turiel, E., and G. Rothman. 1972. "The Influence on Behavioral Choices at Different Stages of Moral Development." Child Development 43: 741-56.

Werner, H. 1957. Comparative Psychology of Mental Development. New York: International Universities Press.

Werner, P. 1976. "A Canonical Correlation Analysis of Beliefs and Attitudes Regarding Abortion." Paper presented at the 56th Annual Convention of the Western Psychological Association, Los Angeles.

Weston, D., and E. Turiel. 1980. "Act-Rule Relations: Children's Concepts of Social Rules." Developmental Psychology 16: 417-24.

Whiting, J. W. M. 1960. "Resource Mediation and Learning by Identification." In Personality Development in Children, edited by I. Iscoe and H. W. Stevenson. Austin: University of Texas Press.

Wolfson, A. 1972. "Aspects of the Development of Identity Concepts." Ph.D. dissertation, University of California, Berkeley.

Zellman, G. L., A. Leibowitz, M. Eisen, and J. R. Evans. 1980. "Adolescent Pregnancy Decision Making." Paper presented at the annual meeting of the Western Psychological Association, Honolulu.

Zelnik, M., and J. F. Kantner. 1980. "Sexual Activity, Contraceptive Use, and Pregnancy among Metropolitan Teenagers: 1971-1979." Family Planning Perspectives 12: 230-37.

INDEX

Abernathy, V., 3, 7
Adler, N., 3, 6, 7
age, 26, 88, 117, 130
Arney, W. R., 3
Aronfreed, 9
attitudes, 4, 5, 85, 87, 92, 113, 137

Baldwin, W., 7
Bandura, A., 9
Barglow, P., 3
Belenky, M. F., 5, 22, 23, 88
Beswick, D. G., 5
Blasi, A., 63
Bracken, M. B., 3, 4, 6
Broughton, J., 21
Buss, A., 78

Callahan, D., 2
Cheyne, J. A., 9
classification task, 57–58, 88, 113–16
clinical interview, about abortion, 27, 88, 119; method of, 27; about overpopulation, 132
Colby, A., 14
conflict, 87–88; and domain change, 86; and reasoning about abortion, 54, 75, 87, 130; and stage change, 86
confusion and reasoning about abortion, 55, 56, 76, 129–30
contraceptive use, 6, 120, 122
coordinated dilemma, 131, 134
coordinated reasoning, 50–54, 97–103, 128–29; and action choices, 74–75, 77

counseling services, 138
countersuggestion, 28, 41

Damon, W., 22, 80, 136
decision-making models, 6
DeMersseman, S. A., 136
Diamond, M., 4
domain, 10–11; and action choices, 63, 77, 83; change of, 86, 112–13; confusions of, 22–23, 136–37; coordinations of, 11, 46, 50–54, 133, 137; distinctions of, 11, 22–25, 57, 83, 136

education: background, 80, 81, 82; level, 26, 88; programs, 129, 138
Elkind, D., 21
equilibration, 86, 112–13
Erikson, E., 7
Evans, J. R., 4, 81

Fischman, S., 4
Flavell, J. H., 10
Ford, C., 2, 87
Freeman, E., 3
Freud, A., 7
Furth, H. G., 79

Gibbs, J., 15
Gilligan, C., 5, 23, 88, 118
Goldsmith, S., 4
Gordon, N. J., 21

ABOUT THE AUTHOR

JUDITH SMETANA is Assistant Professor of Education, Psychology, and Pediatrics at the University of Rochester, Rochester, New York. During 1978/79 she held a postdoctoral fellowship in Psychology at the University of Michigan.

Dr. Smetana has published in the areas of social and moral development and adolescent-pregnancy decision making.

Dr. Smetana holds a B.A. from the University of California at Berkeley and an M.S. and Ph.D. from the University of California at Santa Cruz.

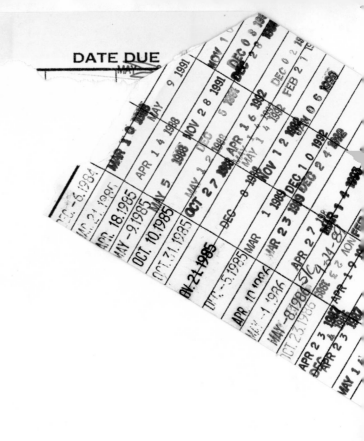